Contents

VOL 93 NO 2 SUMMER 20

Poems

Essays

Reviews

Poet in the Gallery

Art

Poems

Don Paterson

THE READING

The first time I came to your wandering attention
my name was Simonides. Poets,
whose air of ingratitude forms in the womb
have reason at least to thank me:
I invented the thing you now call the commission.
Oh – and one other frivolity
refined by Aquinas, tuned up by Bruno
and perfected by Hannibal Lecter.

All in good time. But first to the theme
of this evening's address: the reading.
It was not a good poem, if I say so myself.
As good as the fee, though, and better
than him who that day bought my praises: a man
of so little virtue to sing of
I ended up fleshing it out, as you do,
with something I'd found in the drawer –

a hymn that I'd made a while back, for the twin sons
of Leda, the Dioscuri.
At the feast he had held in his own dubious honour
the little king signed me to start;
but though they were quiet for my halfbaked encomium –
applauding like seals when I'd finished –
his guests, when I started to read from my own stuff,
returned to their wolfing and hollering.

The king, though, was silent. My lyric economies
had not, so it seemed, gone unnoticed.
When he offered me only one-half the struck price,
I made too much show of my anger
knowing, I dare say, his wrath the more just –
but right then I seemed to go deaf;
every eye turned on me, narrowed – at which point
I thought it a smart move to drop it.

However, I fixed each man's face in my mind,
each man at his rank at the table
(that trick of mine; your coupons, O my rapt listeners,
I'll have nailed by the end of this poem).
Then this. A young slave-girl ran into the hall
then right up to me, with this message:
two golden-haired boys had arrived at the gate,
and wanted to talk with me. Urgently.

I asked that I might be excused, a small boon
they were more than delighted to grant,
and took a slow stroll to the gate. I found no one;
bloody kids. I turned back to the hall
and cursed them to heaven. Heaven replied
without hesitation or stint: a great thunderbolt
aimed not at me, but the ridgepole.
The roof groaned and splintered, sagged for a moment
then cracked, and came down on the lot of them.

After the dust and the sirens had died
the wives all came wailing and weeping
to claim what they could of their tenderised menfolk.
Alas, they were all so disfigured
no-one could work out whose husband was whose.
Of course I could. *The redbeard? Just there,*
by the fire. And the scarface? The door. And the hawknose?
Poor woman: look under your feet.

I picked my way down to head of the table
and held the fixed gaze of my patron
as I knelt in the rafters and carefully counted
the rest of my fee from his purse.

THE SHUT-IN

Good of them, all told, to leave me locked
inside my favourite hour: the whole one early
I came to wait for one I loved too dearly
in this coffered snug below the viaduct
with my dark vernacular ale, Stevenson's
short fiction, and the little game I played
of not thinking of her, except to thumb away
the exquisite stitch that gathers at my breastbone.

The minute hand strains at its lengthening tether
like Achilles on the hare; the luscious beer
refills; the millionth page flowers on the last
of *The Bottle Imp...* O Fathers, leave me here,
beyond the night, the stars, beyond the vast
infinitesimal letdown of each other!

Simon Carnell

FACE AT THE GLASS

The ribbed glass in the door
gave the face pressed against it staring in
a radical, cubistic distortion.
A straggle of beard and an outsize eye.
The hair of someone dragged through a hedge
backwards. And then again, forwards.
A few remaining teeth, doing their own thing.
This could be "John", author of the cryptic note,
the first non-threatening mail you found
on the doormat of the newly rented house:
YOU DONT NO ME BUT COULD YOU LEND
A POUND 50. DONT TELL ALFRED.
Alfred you didn't know from Adam.
Once inside, the eyes were still going
in two disconcertingly different directions,
neither of them the one in which you stood.
John who was interested in having
the TO LET sign for firewood or no reason.
John who pushed a handcart up and down
the main road into Leeds, filling it with dreck.
John who was beaten up and urinated on
in the park, and who lived around the corner
with his also "heavily medicated" brother
who sent him out to glean
small amounts of cash. *Now then John,*
you don't want to be borrowing
and not paying back. Now then John . . .
John did both sides of the conversation.
Beetling away from the house gesticulating,
with one pound fifty, an apple, an orange
and a loaf of Mother's Pride.

In winter he had Kwik Save carriers
for improvised overshoes,
and a curious pair of castoffs: dandy
yellow loon pants: part of somebody else's idea
of Care In The Community.
Your own life edging sideways into parenthesis . . .
Months in front of an open fire in the kitchen,
then close up to the pond life in the derelict garden;
one piece of aimless reading – *The Unnamable* –
leading to another – "Project For a Homeless Vehicle" –
with its sort of supermarket trolley
capable of transforming
into a bunk, a barbecue, or a bicycle.
You couldn't get down this street without
a thumbs-up from Monica, on the *qui vive*,
behind bottle-thick bi-focals and net
half-curtain, half her other eye
on a blizzard of malfunctioning TV
– and marvelled at the dialogue
that could be got going, and as easily de-railed:
on neighbours, local history,
and the naming of dogs.
This damp valley was teeming with snails,
and your black whippet-thin lurcher
rescued from the dog-pound, ate snails,
craving the calcium in their sick-making shells.
Now then sir, now then sir –
you must lurch after him
before he can get to lurch after them.
So what did you think you were doing
– a knock at the door, the face at the glass –
dropping to the floor, going out of the room
on all fours, pretending not to be home?

HOTEL MADRAS

In a Madras cold water hotel room with intermittent cold water –
a bucket for a shower – the delicately carved wooden shutters
opening onto a piece of baked waste ground

with its painted cow and smaller cattle (skeletal yellow dog with
withered hind legs, dragging the dead half of itself like a biped
in a grafted-on cart) you prepare a scene

of erotic welcome: a threshold of intricately chalked decorations
– marked with the same tear-shaped signature motif you doodled,
when phoning, on scraps of squared paper

– and a pale blue box of unnaturally coloured sweets, patterned
in your absence by tiny sugar-powered ants, working their lines
of busy two-way traffic. A *muezzin* cried

through a microphone. Your chameleon voice had taken on an
Anglo-Indian intonation. In the Nilgiri hills, the children rushed
to meet us calling you – "Miss Erica" –

from the schoolroom; the school's missionary owners the kind
who'd forbidden builders a *drishti* to fend evil from the rooms
on which they worked – and lacking this

scarecrow-like figure lost a man, who fell from the scaffolding
and broke his neck. Italian, in a sari, schooled by Mrs Sashikala
whose near-black face and too low caste

made her unwelcome even in the hotel foyer, you'd been living
your girlhood dream of India; happier than in the long descent
into England, which you'd begun lying

anorexic in a high-rise hospital in Hong Kong, reading all of fat
Dickens. To see the immense spirit of the poor. Living cutting
                    sandals out of car tyres; biking to stalls

cut blocks of ice; pavement barbers, dentists; a small girl leading
her blind father to beg through aisles of unmoved bus passengers.
                    The leper holding up five half-gone fingers

to glassless windows. And the quadruple amputee with a drum
between his teeth, writhing to play it with clappers on strings –
                    – fortunate, since the system has a still lower

floor. The water buffalo looked prehistoric but at home: horns
just visible parallel to the black water's surface, sunk in a river
                    become the city's high summer sewer.

And the bright gods not lacking offerings of flowers. And you,
with some of the poorest women, wearing a string of tightly
                    budded fresh jasmine flowers in your hair.

Carrie Etter

FIN DE SIÉCLE

It's not that the water isn't potable, but only a few stars come down to earth now, and by ones and threes opera-goers linger in the dark house. They settle back into their seats around midnight, staring forward as though an encore will soon begin. Afternoons, children sit on the ground next to the birch, positioning themselves so that if they were but eight feet higher, they'd perch on the five stout boughs hacked to stumps last week. They try to perfect a way of slackening their legs, now drooping, now bending, but their legs will not dangle and swing. The grandfather hastens the children home yet remains after they are gone, gazing at the invisible boughs and reaching up as though he would brush the bark with his fingertips, if he were just tall enough.

ESCALATION

for Lytton Smith

If the river narrows, my craft widens at the affront. It may pretend merely to have exhaled too fully, too long, but I would not have you deceived. Does my tiara of cranberry branches look bitter? Do you take another sip of lager each time the newscaster says "weapons of mass destruction"? I asked you here to act as cache for my ruby ring and my port-induced hangover. The invitation alone obligates you to explain to me "non-civilian target," or better yet, "acceptable casualties." The din is closing. Make your promises before it stops your ears.

PATHETIC FALLACY AS NECESSARY

The drone and occasional shriek arise not from a hive,
but a cantankerous machine, its hypochondria
in full swing despite persistent neglect.

After all, the hometown offers no other buzz,
unless you reckon the glee of dizzied consumers
clicking and clucking through the winding mall.

"I've been teaching math all my life without
reading one of these philosophers of it," says the retiree
two tables over. "Why start now?"

Robert Saxton

THE BOOK OF DAYS

On distant farms where brawns are bred
we quislings learn to quench our qualms.
We breakfast royally, in bed,
at ease on distant farms.

The good life snakes its ample charms
through all that's thought and all that's said.
At beggar-my-dog The Weightwatcher's Arms

annihilates The Angler's Head.
To the faint music of distant alarms
we ruminate, ill-kempt, well-fed,
at ease on distant farms.

* * *

In shepherd's caves, redemption-bound,
we shelter while the shepherd shaves,
hoping our luck won't turn around,
happy in shepherd's caves.

Our shepherd, like an angel, braves
a scything flood that wakes his wound.
At blast-my-soul The Prince of Graves

humiliates The Nymph Aground.
We sing amid the worsening waves,
safe and dry where sheep have drowned,
happy in shepherd's caves.

* * *

On windless fells in bowls of scree
    we yodellers yomp our yearning yells
from crag to crag, exhausted, free,
        walking on windless fells.

We hump in fields of asphodels,
    declaring our love belatedly.
At jolly-my-gum The Cockleshells

eliminates The Milking Tree.
    Our water comes from streams, not wells,
and keeps our spirits up, like tea,
        walking on windless fells.

* * *

Above the bay, wave-lashing rocks,
    the West wind leads our wits astray,
like wayward stragglers from flocks
        of gulls above the bay

where, ten to the dozen, dolphins play,
    maddened by the equinox.
At slack-man's-pride The Old Cathay

exterminates The Wily Fox.
    We've given our worldly goods away,
exchanging wives and quilts and clocks
        for gulls above the bay.

* * *

Out in the straits a holy mill
    of light through noise of night pulsates
to flash the news, we're praying still,
        on our rock out in the straits.

One lighthouse now accommodates
    the city of God, and does God's will.
At dibble-my-dock The William Gates

embarrasses The Shepherdess.
    Our treadwheel groaningly rotates
to strip of its perilous black dress
        our rock out in the straits.

THE INCENDIARY GHOST'S CONVERSION

When two people meet who have slept with a third,
at different times of life, to neither's knowledge,
the room adjusts its mood to a drop in the pressure of destiny,
like a lone pilgrim who reaches a fork in the road,
such a relief after many miles of arduous walking –
an interesting place at last, and one that offers a kind of peace.

What keeps this revelation at bay as the friendship blossoms,
the mischief always managing to dodge just out of sight?
There's always a danger zone in which we share
our happiest moments while the ghost flaps unseen in its box,
or elsewhere, busy around others, fanning, not quietening, a flame
of untoward kinship, occasionally setting curtains on fire.

This happened once to me. I paddled at the blaze with my hands.
Things half-destroyed are terrible, rioting against our wish
for them to disappear entirely. Somehow I settled
into my flesh again, made good the room, and brought a woman
back, first of those two. After months of intricate debate
we stumbled upon the umbilical proof of the existence of love.

Alison Brackenbury

LOOKING THROUGH

I read newspapers, endlessly,
when I should be doing
so many things. The actresses are best
in the obituaries: their tiny bones,
their triple marriages. How often they end up
with a dog, upon a ranch, alone.

What does this tell me, about women,
even about dogs? Nothing.
It is the soul
which loves to look at mountains, in clear air.

Sarah Maguire

A FISTFUL OF FORAMINIFERA

Sand, at first glance –
granular,

a rich grist
of grains and slim seeds,

opening
into a swarm of small homes

painted rose or ochre, saffron, chalk,
some blown steady as glass –

hyaline, diamond,
the pellucid private chamber of a tear.

*   *   *   *

The balanced simplicity of a singlecelled cell,
busy with its business

in absolute silence.
Pseudopodia

float
clear through their apertures,

banners coursing the waters,
furbelows, scarves, ragged skirts;

brief tactful netting,
shy gestures of touch.

Their filigree mansions
are chambered with secrets –

auricular passageways
give onto galleries,

soft arcades,
furrowed with arbours, open

onto balconies, that lean
over doors, propped ajar.

*   *   *   *

Benthic,
their galaxies carpet the depths of the oceans,

a slow chalky ooze
bedded down softly in darkness.

They conjure their houses
from flotsam and jetsam,

tucking grains closely
between alveoli,

secreting a hardy, calcareous mortar;
the shell walls buffed till they shine

or pebbledashed sugary white –
the architectonics of happenstance and grace.

*   *   *   *

Pennies from heaven,
the yellowing bedrock

hewn into slabs
is stuffed full of treasures.

Slipped from their homes
come hundreds of coins,

big stumbling sovereigns,
pocketfuls of pocketmoney,

fit for flipping, fit for hoarding
in chests.

Nummulites gizahensis,
the wealth of the pharaohs

is hauled up heavenwards,
a limestone staircase to the stars.

* * * *

Tumbleweeds, spacecraft, seedpearls, squid,
fairylights, pincushions, biodomes, sheaths,

colanders, starfish, thistledown, dhal,
powderpuffs, ammonites, cornichons, teeth,

puffballs, longbones, condoms, bulbs,
thermometers, pomegranates, catapults, hail.

* * * *

Open your fists
and the mortal remains of one million creatures

will spill
through your fingers –

Eocene
dust in the wind.

Richard Price

SLOW FILMS

A few long films

from the seventies –
there are no better.

That's not right.
"Are there any better?"

I like

three or four
slow films,

the sixties,
the seventies,

I think.

They take their time.
They don't take yours.

John Wilkinson

FOUR POEMS

Mercator

A lovers' shadow, thumbed
from waxy & ambitious
skins advances to the knoll,
casts its bolt, sees eye to eye,

the sticking place is always
darling that reluctant
ever to seal over, coercive
pulls their troubled shade.

Merry co-star will deflect
as though impregnable,
spot spent position-taking
startles to the bigness there,

taps the shadowy mound
loosening caught heels.
Darling sweat the loud
thunder, let its rolls extend

crescendo on crescendo,
flattening a carefully-cut
circle. In San Diego, loaded
sequencers conceive cells.

Dateline

Fingers move across the buttons
in all-there, in nothing-doing,
am they being spoken to.
If you want help, go to the back wall,
in the one-person capsule
to the touch screen. Forensics
cleans up your footprint departed.

Alone they work in concert.
Without betraying a word, they work –
is that an improvised runway? Is
to the same end, is that blood?
that a gang-attack? It saw a severed
head below the elder bush,
or am I a report recently launched?

Save that for your usual outburst:
there in the world, boulders of lint
shine, make clattering noises,
names are dropped, people dropped,
policies dropped, special effects
run the mill. Internal
motivation gallops in sealed units.

Abacus

A touch looped so to rest
constituted, which by maul
content, touched-on it
betrays. Geranium
traffic drips off the rain,

out of sight out of mind
steeply that it might linger.
Foxglove fingers
snuggling the figures
made for its drops to veer:

pray all activity heed
the one account, divining
bones, the turbid sky
slipping its distillate
from wire to wire, touch

paper, touchstone. What
was had by drip-feed,
run-off of the one
instalment, padding bones,
rolls in immaculate skin.

Squared Off

This is the same room, equable,
to itemize is not to have returned
stuffed with things ill-recollected
either upon this stele, or bellywise.

Are these the surroundings to love,
here were shaken down, frayed
or are they not let in? The things
leather, tarnished smiles, cold hands

scrabbling at valves but intermit,
bury vials during gaps in flow –
re-pump a negative pressure room.
Spins the stylus, floats the pointer,

taking stock of surroundings: are
things in their place, in balance –
favourite persons once counted out,
objects for distraint, sequestered?

Julian Stannard

PIAZZA DELLA POSTA VECCHIA

Darling, they've dripped gold lights over our piazza,
the knocking shop of our glorious epoch
where the Borgia Prince *Bettino Craxi*
once hovered in the courtyard
buoyed up by a hit squad of squeaking puppets.
We peeped out naked, so sexually wired.
Come back to bed, you said.
That's when I noticed we didn't actually *have* a bed.

DEA EX MACHINA

A hand taps me on the shoulder
in that shockless dive near *Principe*.
I turn to find the mysterious Maude.
She's wonderful when she's in a dither.
We kiss, kiss, kiss and kiss again.
In that bag, she says, I've got
a perfectly healthy cheque book.
Only say the word, just say it, *damn you . . .*

Antony Dunn

KITCHEN SINK DRAMA

On the one hand, this
is Mark, washing up.

But see here, beyond the pane
above the altar-ware of taps,

that spider again, slubbing
its train of leadwork around the frame,

maker and mender, restless heart
of its own rose window;

libations of rain, spiced
with sulphides and soot,

the transubstantiation of frost
and sun, puzzling out shards of colour;

this work holding house and home
together. So, on the other hand,

this is Mark, offering
his forgetful hands –

a pair of doves –
in a cage of water and knives.

Polly Clark

HEDGEHOG

Its leg was not broken. It was not homeless.
It clenched in my hands, a living flinch.
You cannot love so much and live,
it whispered, its spines clicking like teeth.
I hid it from itself in a cardboard box.

Overnight it nibbled a hole and slipped away.
I cried so much my mother thought I'd never stop.
She said, *you cannot love so* – and yet
I grew to average size and amused a lot of people
with my prickliness and brilliant escapes.

Jane Griffiths

from ICARUS ON EARTH

Mother

A kind of metamorphosis. His arm
twists fishlike through my fingers,
he lives outside, cries like a gannet,
shears through raspberry canes and
pampas grass for whole Sundays
shuttered in the tree-house. The cat
comes in feathered and tarred.

Still worse, the things I've overheard:
how he one-legged along the parapet,
head skied, arms spread-eagled, and
trainspotting, he said, till they talked
him down. And now, when I bend
to kiss him I see in the August blue
of his eyes not myself, inverted, but

a soft flicker as when we swim
under the viaduct: joint jack and kick
of our long-legged spines, overarm
reach parting doubled nets of birch
and the rush a kind of cradling.
Tap and pulse of our feet against
the current's shaled strata invisible

till he lights out in a rivulet
arrowhead, a catch in my body's
smooth casket waving
from the bridge and I
am watching the sky webbed
and sinuous between his fingers,
arms flexed to my sides,

treading water like lead.

Girl

What I remember is this: the afternoon
running out in long grasses, the quick white
root system of our fingers and their slender
hold on the earth, the afterlife of the worm.

The word *loam*, the sharp sand edging
the pit, ten strong carapaces of nails chocked
with grime: digging for Australia, digging
for the island, and up to the elbows in it.

The bird's eye view: cavern of dock leaves,
borage a masthead startled through
the ribbing and into skyblue gravity over
my nose and cheekbone among reeds

in the pond, a leg kicking between branches.
Caustic grain of brick against the skin
and on my knee an exopthalmic jewel
of blood, a toad's eye darkling. Arc

and spring of the pearl-handled penknife
in my palm. On the wide stone ledge
static of a dragonfly breaking its flight.
The pelt of sunlight ruffled on my back.

Icarus

As it is in books, when, Friday afternoons,
the plimsoll-footed teacher hands down
reading time and the four walls
of the classroom quiver and fall
away as a springboard clappers, a diver
soars, or the father comes home
from the factory and brings a kite,
perfect strung wings,

and the long lines of print glide and brim
like gulls in formation or in battery:
waves over a dazzle of white whose
wax-coated covers take to the hands
like wings so my feet are digging the soft
sift of sand, the sharps of shellfish;
I've a graft of feathers like tattoos
under the skin,

the taut of struts in a kite's casing
as it lifts: a ribcage of air,
a mote skied in the stairwell on
its ascent long and stepped as a lifeline
when I turn from the page as from the world
under my wing as if there were no known
end to it, when the kite castles in air as if
there were no strings.

Girl

What I remember is this –
that you called me in the long fall-out
of an autumn Sunday, the kiss

of leaves turning in the park, creak
of branches the leather hinging of rooks
on take-off or the sign for Welwyn, Palmer's Green.

How we were on top of the world
and our shadows' crossed purposes, trod the earth
under and fell windstopped

and laughing at the top of the escarpment.
How the common ground cut below the pale
as if there'd be no end to it and

the train on the viaduct beneath our feet
shook up the green as the wind
pulses through long grasses and we

hung against post and rail in diapason
giving slip to its slipstream. How
we went under and drew the sun

down and round with us. It was
early dark. Like a meteor a train
came out over the moon and rattled the stars

from Orion. You knew a way out,
you said; you said you walked all night
with the feathers I gave you twisting about

and about again against your palm
like radar, a rudder, the two-pronged
wooden fork of divination.

Now you write with the weight of the Atlantic
behind you that even the stars look different.
So I could tell you I hunch the height

of ocean against the skyline, that I drove
out tonight and the streetlights spun
constellar over the road.

That I would give you the earth
in a handful of signs – tilt against Kansas, Illinois
Hitchin; Hertford; Hatfield and the north.

Biographer

If it had been a different island, less green,
less grey. If there had been no hedges, no
litany of trains fluent in the liquid
air, no rain cradling the echo as a bubble
about to burst. No movement. No past.
No Sundays in the greenhouse taking up
roots and putting them down again.
If it had been a different cross-section
of earth against the glass. If the laws of
gravity had gone west, if there'd been
no books to tell us about them, vicarious,
flipped pages dipping like island on
island below the horizon, prodigal as if
there'd been nothing new under the sun:
island on island dipping below the horizon,
flipped pages prodigal to tell us about them.
Or if there'd been no books to show how
the balled earth bends gravity to its laws.
If the crossing had been sectioned off,
the sun past movement behind glass.
No. Sunday a greenhouse, a cradle,
a bubble about to burst in the rain.
Putting down roots and taking them up,
the air liquid, and fluent as an echo
its litany of grey, hedges, green
going west with the trains, vicarious –
no less if it had been a different island.

Tom Payne

TAPIRS FOR CAMILLE SAINT-SAËNS

If he hadn't gone for some of the steadier creatures already
        such as the elephant, Camille Saint-Saëns could have done
with a trot for the tapirs in his carnival.
        Two bassoons for these monogamous types,
gently honking to conjure proboscises,
        the second following the first in tidy canon.
No need to change key much; the trick would be
        to find a tune to play, then play it back again,
the shnozz of the one nudging the other's tush.
        No need, either, to worry that we don't know
what noise a tapir makes (we're happy after all
        for the tortoise to be silent if the can-can sets him kicking):
a pause between movements would give us a chance
        to share in the tapirs' calm and droopy wonder.

Jon Woodward

TWO POEMS

your eyes are just hanging
there in their closets candy
coating would do them some
good hell candy coating would
be a real boon for

us all this morning when
I woke up I fabricated
the following nightmare you dangled
a microphone from your teeth
you were on a ledge

four stories up the microphone
swung back and forth I
was jumping trying to grasp
it whaddaya mean not scary
I'll show you not scary

I have to think up
things to say ahead of
time to keep from stuttering
when I speak it's the
only thing that works I've

got a brain full of
index cards you'd be appalled
unfortunately what I memorize becomes
obsolete almost immediately the conversation
goes unforeseeable places by the

time I got on the
bus it was raining and
it probably rained on you
as you walked home anyway
and I'm sorry about that too

Moniza Alvi

CASTAWAY
after Jules Supervielle

A table quite near to us and a faraway lamp
can't be linked up again in the hostile air.
And right up to the skyline – an empty beach.
A man in the sea is waving, screaming *Help!*
and his echo replies *What do you mean by that?*

WHISPER IN AGONY

after Jules Supervielle

No need to be shocked.
Close your eyelids until
they harden into stone.

Disregard your heart
even if it stops.
It only beats for itself
on its private slope.

Your hands will stretch out
in their boats of ice
and your forehead will be blank
as a vast empty square
that separates two armies.

MOVEMENT
after Jules Supervielle

The horse that turned its head,
saw what no one has ever seen,
then carried on grazing
in the shade of the eucalyptus.

It wasn't a person or a tree.
It wasn't a mare,
nor even a memory of the wind
exercising in the foliage.

It's what another horse
suddenly turned its head
and glimpsed at that same hour
twenty thousand centuries ago,

and what no being will see again,
not man, horse, fish, insect –
until the soil is reduced
to a crumbled statue
without arms, legs or head.

Miklós Radnóti

NEITHER MEMORY, NOR MAGIC

There was all that anger hidden here in my heart before,
As the seeds dark as Africans hide in an apple-core,
And I knew there was an angel walking, sword in hand, behind me –
There in my time of trouble to guard me and defend me.
But if, some wild dawn hour, you should awake to find
Your world in ruins and, your few things left behind,
Should set forth almost naked, a ghost in the dawn glow –
Then in your fine and lightly-pacing heart there'll start to grow
A mature humility, reflective, sparing of speech;
When you do speak rebellion, it'll be disinterested
And in hope of a free future shining from far ahead.

I never did have anything and never shall do now.
Consider for a moment how wealthy my life is, how
Little I seek revenge, there being no anger in my heart;
The world will be rebuilt and where the new walls start
My song, which is now banned, will be heard again, my voice.
I live through in myself all that will come to pass.
I shall look back no more, for I know: nothing can save me,
Neither memory, nor magic – the sky lours above me.
Friend, if you see me, shrug, then turn your back on me.
Where the angel with his sword was standing once
There may be nobody.

Translated by Clive Wilmer and George Gömöri

Robert Chandler

ELENA

If your sister mentions your name, what I hear is always a story you told us that evening,

The story of how, after you had moved to Tashkent – Russian father, American mother, and you were born in China,

And in 1956 you had all gone back to the USSR, what with your father suffering toskà for the motherland

And your sister, Nadezhda, meaning 'Hope', dreaming she could contribute, with her knowledge of languages,

To international understanding – what I hear is how, in Tashkent, a city your grandfather, General Bitov,

Had once conquered for Tsar Nikolay, but where you now all lived in one room, since your holy fool of a father

Had entrusted to GosBank all the dollars he had saved during thirty years reluctantly trading timber,

And where you were trapped, since the USSR, then as ever, was easier to get into than out of,

And the only blessing was that the Russian Consul in Tsientsyn had had the grace to dissuade your father,

Playing on his worries over baby Misha's asthma, and the cold, and the journey, from returning before Stalin's death,

In which case you would all have been shot, or scattered around the Gulag – yes, what I hear is how, in Tashkent,

Your mother once boiled some valerian root to tide you over who knows what upset, and while it was cooling,

The liquid was drunk by the cat, who then slipped into the cupboard containing precious teacups from China,

Your family's last link with a world now lost for ever, and the cat, crazed by the valerian,

Was unable to find its way out of the cupboard and began to charge round in circles, pulverising the china

And so aggravating its panic, which made it charge faster, weaving together this story I always remember you by.

Roger Waterfield

DOMESTIC

The eyes of a mouse
in a trap; open and bright,
looking straight at you.

Family cars have
cat footprints on the bonnet
(replace as desired).

Do I feed the birds?
Yes, I scatter a balanced
diet for the worms.

And do I love you?
Yes, I write letters to MAFF
and the D.T.I.

This is the widest
house in the world. It stretches
from my bed to yours.

John Kinsella

FATIGUES

It's astonishing how connections
are suppressed as the square men in peaked hats
and fatigues let the body – the carcass – of a stag
drop over the tailgate of a four-by-four pick-up,
no sissy SUV, but a monster like an F250, gloating like the strip
of glittering advertising that runs across the base
of the cable TV broadcast, self-advertising, smug
parody of itself;
two Amish men – twins it would seem –
no more than late teens or early twenties, shopping
for glow-flighted arrows and pretzels from Walmart,
their buggy parked in a distant corner
of the car park,
as if they don't mind walking out past the cars,
the horse
shitting behind its blinkers.
Looking for another entry point
to the Kokosing trail, we happen on Danville. Katherine
mis-remembers it as the anchor-point of a school bike excursion.
A pick-up in the car park celebrates bow hunting –
a luminous
sticker. The town reminds us of somewhere in the South-west
of Australia, say Bridgetown where I lived for a year
and was run out with my friends because we were
"hippy shits" and "dyke-fleas", where our water
was poisoned
and a town roo-shooter watched from highground,
binoculars
glinting in the setting sun, incarcerated in brittle
cold air –
yes, I keep bringing this up, but it can't
be written out in a few metrically neat stanzas,

especially
in a beat that neither the shooter nor his intended victims
would recognise. Incidentally, bunches or clusters
of men leave from the city for such expeditions,
so it's not just of the country, though most see
it as a country thing.
In Washington DC and northern
Virginia a sniper is game-playing – Fox Media,
with *gusto*, conveys death, describes death as "picking them off",
and talks in terms of "headshots". They interview
hunters on shooting ranges, the season opening. The NRA
don't want the signatures of gun-barrels to be written
into a DNA record;
I have been around roo shooters
and cat killers and have myself killed birds and foxes and rabbits
and fish and insects;
I have also killed a ram
with a broken neck. That's well over twenty years ago: I say
this so you know that I know what I'm talking about.
Images
are scarce or toxic,
blurred by the changing season.
Blood
mingles with altering leaf-colour,
red fall-through,
glowing in the fallout of open fires,
illuminating
the village taxidermist's. The art of these lines
is to show no animal feeling. My blood might be
tainted, but I'm probably not human. Maybe utterance
traps me,
"hunter"/poet, sacerdotal flasher:
understand
that these killers might see miracles too, and experience
God's love, and have their prayers listened to.

But what they
offer in return – God so reliant on goodwill – is confused,
is an hallucination weighed down with the addictive
taste of plasma and red corpuscles,
anointed communities
focussed through crosshairs at turkey shoots and fox hunts
and rabbit kills, cultural preservatives that kill them slowly,
anecdotal as inheritance, familial polyps
sticking out like bad beacons,
kids feeling the rush differently
and obviously wanting more.
When the light's
not quite right in the scope
a faun can become a witch, a bad spirit;
alcohol
is not essential – fizzy drinks full of sugar
do a similar thing,
these trees and hands
marked by powder burns,
paying homage
to the dead they never knew.

Peter Finch

LLYWELYN GOCH AP MEURIG HEN AT SPEED

South heart like a birchtop woodsong
light and little proud ah
Lleucu heart broken
Merioneth
Machynlleth
Mawddwy

Deheubarth buggered

the barbs of longing the pain

You've been writing again, she said,
no it's just blisters on my fingertips,
and great caves in
the space inside me. Heart
thinks it's the soul. Full of birds.

Life has five plots:
rise to fame, fall from grace,
gain love, lose it
and death.

Nick Laird

THE BEARHUG

It's not as if I'm intending on spending the rest of my life doing this:
besuited, rebooted, filing to work, this poem a fishbone in my briefcase.
The scaffolding clinging St Paul's is less urban ivy than skin, peeling off.

A singular sprinkler shaking his head spits at the newsprint of birdshit.
It's going unread: Gooseberry Poptarts, stale wheaten bread, Nutella and toothpaste.
An open-armed crane offers sexual favours to aeroplanes passing above.

I hadn't the foggiest notion. Imagine: me, munching cardboard and rubbish,
but that's just what they meant when they said, *Come in, you're dead-beat,*
take the weight off your paws, you're a big weary grizzly with a hook through his
mouth,

here, have some of this love.

DISCLAIMER

Know who picks this up will write me out.

Know this time clamour could be tactical.
Every hand-held, tell-tale poem
is a little underwritten by intended art

though I bypassed round the heart of town,
skipped articulated sorries, the adjectival pile-ups,
and got foxed instead by variance:

inflammable's prefix, the definitions of cleave,
how a breadman shot, point blank, in the neck
scatters loaves on the tarmac like meanings,

to where this room is dark, then morninged with light,
and slowed with the uncentred difference of absence.
Know whilst any resemblance may be purely luck,

by writing it down he wrote you in.

THE RETURN OF THE ALTERNATIVE

North, for instance, does not mean good – James Fenton

Its morning fag left casually to smoulder
on the broken saucer of the sky,
dawn yawns birdsong, then coughs exhausts.

Another panicked night awake.
I wash and shuffle from the bath
and shiver off like someone pulled aboard.

The plumbing's sighs are almost human.
I glimpse myself – exhausted, slick,
a bag of nerves and urgencies.

For once if I could stop myself in time
I would unwind and cut me down to size,
in half, to four, then eight, sixteen,

and try the lives that happened elsewhere.
Smoke trails from mouths as if from planes
and the sun grows ash.

DONE

We've come to bag the evidence.
This might be the scene of a murder.
Dustsheets and silence and blame.

The flat empties its stomach into the hall.
We have given back letters and eaten our words.
You wrote off the Volvo. I gave you verrucas.

And like the window of a jeweller's after closing
the shelves in the study offer up nothing.
I slowly take the steps down one by one,

and for the first time maybe,
notice the chaos, the smouldering traffic,
the litter, bystanders, what have you

Essays

TOBY LITT

Reading

ONE REVIEWER OF J.K.Rowling's fourth book asked their child what they thought of it. The child said, "It took a while for the book to disappear, but after that it was great". This is the best description I have come across of enraptured reading. The second best comes from Wallace Stevens' poem "The House Was Quiet and the World Was Calm": "The words were spoken as if there was no book". Very strangely, this follows rather than leads up to the more extreme statement that, "The reader became the book". Which, surely, is the most enraptured of all imaginable readings – when the boundaries of personal identity are felt to have dissolved.

Auden famously claimed that the purpose of poetry was to "disenchant"; and at the opposite end of the scale from the disappeared book comes disenchanted reading, the reading of the reader who never forgets the wordiness of the words on the page. Here is a short sentence from Seymour Chatman's *The Later Style of Henry James*, "There are certain identificational marks worth noting, however, namely that (everything else being equal) an indefinite article or possessive pronoun, especially combined with durative or iterative adverbs, suggests the faculty, while a relative clause or a phrase modifying the noun of perception suggests the thing-perceived". This, of course, isn't reading *as such*, it is written-up academic stylistics. But the statistical verbal analysis practised by, say, Shakespeare scholars is a kind of reading, deliberately estranged from anything but the grammatical components of the text. It is reading done by a low-grade computer. Beyond this, the activity ceases to be reading and becomes instead photocopying or printing – a straight, uninterpreted repetition.

Most of my reading takes place towards the balanced middle of these extremes, and as I become more and more the professional reader (books of obligation, books of pay) the experience of raptness becomes rarer. It may be hard for most writers – certainly most literary writers – to countenance the idea, but it is a fact that the majority of readers are only peripherally aware of style. They will form an opinion, definitely, of whether a book is good or bad, and part of this may be dependent upon whether it is to their mind well or badly written; it is very unlikely they will be able to describe how this has technically been achieved – not unless it's just a matter of the words keeping as much as possible out of the way of the action. (Perhaps this is the difference between literary and non-literary writers: the literary expect to be admired as stylists, the non-literary to be rewarded for absenting themselves.) As a reader, in terms of style, I feel I have become overconscious of how everything is done. If I want to know what it is to be an amateur again, I have to listen to complex music – pop won't do.

Reading is one of the hardest human experiences upon which to report. And I have deliberately avoided going to academic textbooks, because I've hoped to write of it in as experiential a way as I can. There is a scene in the movie of *Fame* where hapless wannabe Doris Schwarz is sat with the dinner her mother has cooked. During her most recent acting lesson, the teacher has advised all the students to observe themselves as they go about the day-to-day business of living. Doris, the model student, tries to watch herself as she eats a forkful of mashed potato. Of course, as we watch her doing this, watching herself, it is the most grotesque and stilted mouthful we have ever seen. When trying to observe myself in the moment of reading, I turn into a kind of verbal Doris: although I know that moving my eyes left to right across the page (my fork from plate to mouth) is what I usually do when reading, I am far more aware that what I am doing is nothing like it normally is.

These, as well as I can remember them, are the things I am most conscious of whilst reading (prose): *the situation* at this point in the book – in a novel, the plot, in biography, the stage of the subject's life, in history, the power-relations, in philosophy, of argument, etc.; *the situation beyond the situation*, or the things which have already occurred, the things I expected would occur but didn't and the things I expect will occur; *the general mood* of the book; *the words* being used to depict the situation; the words as they would sound were I to read them out loud; the words as they impress themselves visually upon me (do any of the coming paragraphs contain dialogue? If so, the characters who haven't been speaking are just about to start to); *the book itself*, physically – its weight, the quality of the paper (perhaps granular, pulpy and hard to read in oblique light); the relative thickness of the book ahead of and behind the open-paged crack in it (Jane Austen plays on this, as with so much else bookish, in *Northanger Abbey* – "The anxiety, which in this state of their attachment must be the portion of Henry and Catherine, and of all who loved either, as to its final event, can hardly extend, I fear, to the bosom of my reader, who will see in the tell-tale compression of the pages before them, that we are all hastening together to perfect felicity"); *the text design*, and how this contributes to or distracts from the reading – widows and orphans, bunchingupinsomeoldertexts; *the typeface* (I can't force myself to read what I think of as the Fay Weldon typeface, used until recently by Sceptre); *the proof-reading* – any typos?; *my body* around the book and most particularly my hands upon it; *my situation*, the physical surroundings, conducive or not, that I find myself in; *the people around me* (sometimes this is equivalent to watching a brilliant production of a great play with a man behind one who sniffs every other minute, wetly); *the necessity of making some kind of aesthetic judgement*, local and general and universal: this choice of word, this shape of phrase, this book; *the author*, and how my reading of this book has formed or altered my impression of them; *my thoughts*, most usually my stray and unwelcome thoughts – of what I have to do later in the day (these are distinct, I'd say, from thoughts called up by the words on the page or the situations described there – memories of similar, unnerving parallel); *my judgements*, usually along the lines of *do I agree – with this metaphor, with this description*?

Poetry is very different. With a poem I usually know exactly where within it I am: it is as if a grid were stencilled upon the page, and I can judge exactly where upon it my eyes are falling. I have a clear idea how many lines I have read, how many are still to come (I will flick ahead to check, if the poem runs over more than a page), and I know how far I am into a line. Poetry is less visually disguised than prose, which can maintain a perfect typographical deadpan even whilst conveying the most devastating news. The typography of a poem is more excitable; it gives itself away, advertises itself in advance. There are, of course, exceptions to this: blank verse offers equally as much opportunity as prose for feeling lost in the page. But these featureless columns are most usually found in modern editions; the originals, with capitalized names, italicized sententiae, abbreviations, ampersands, etc., are likely to be far less proselike – far fuller of visual clues. To make an analogy, prose is a forest, poetry is an ornamental garden – if one gets lost in a poem, it is likely to be in a maze rather than a thicket.

Than prose, the reading of poetry is more guilt-inducing. How can one really live up to, read up to, read with enough committed intelligence and accessible passion, a Shakespeare sonnet? Each reading is inadequate, and none more so than an immediate rereading after a felt-to-be-inadequate first reading. Some poems lift one swiftly to a level of required intensity, Rilke's "Duino Elegies", for example; they force one to fail to disappoint oneself. This is a rare abduction into a verbal world, what Keats refers to as "a little Region to wander in".

I feel distracted and not enough in-the-poem; I've failed it. It's almost as if I haven't read the poem at all, just glanced it through: my eyes haven't entered the black of the words, they've just taken in that they are there on the page

As an experiment, I have decided to reread a poem with which I am familiar, Yeats's "Leda and the Swan". I know, or think I know, the opening lines: "A sudden blow, the great wings beating still / Above the staggering girl, her thighs caressed / By the something something bill / He holds her helpless, breast held to his breast…." About ten years ago, I learnt the poem by heart, and certain phrases have stuck: "her thighs caressed" was unforgettable. And I am aware of the overall shape of the poem, both as a sonnet and as a sonnet by Yeats. There is a certain grandeur both to his endstops and his enjambements; he knows what he's doing, he wants you to know he knows. I think of Rilke and his relationship to Rodin and to Rodin's sculptures; how a poem of Rilke's like "Archaic Torso of Apollo" is Classical sculpture seen through Rodin's eyes. Yeats, similarly, wishes to give a sense of his work having been hewn from stone – of his work having been work. There is a clear sense of previous, less focused, drafts: poems simply do not come out this monumental straight off. I remember reading of a doctor ordering Yeats to stop working, because he'd started to cough up blood. This is the glamour of the unceasing craftsman – of Henry James's hands still moving crablike across the bedsheets, scribbling on his deathbed; of Kafka, unable to speak, still communicating with pencilled notes. With their boots on. I am aware that "Leda and the Swan" is a poem about rape, but that this doesn't bother me all that much – that perhaps it should bother me more; a lot more. Yeats puts a great deal of effort into the descriptions of violence and enforced calm, but it remains mythological and then remythologized violence. What I expect to be feeling, by the end of the poem, is exhilaration; that it hasn't disappointed – it is still as fantastically powerful a verbal construction as I've come to think it. "Leda and the Swan" is a big fat motorbike of a poem, with plenty of horsepower to shoot one off towards the horizon. Afterwards, I will probably want to read more Yeats – his *Greatest Hits*: "Easter, 1919", "Among Schoolchildren", "Byzantium", "Sailing to Byzantium", "The fascination of what's difficult", "The Circus Animals' Desertion". I haven't read a biography of Yeats, so I'm not going to be thinking of the circumstances in which Yeats wrote the poem; but, unless they're built in to a poem, I rarely do. I might think of Wallace Stevens, dictating lines to his secretary at the insurance company, or of Eliot, on Margate Sands, convalescing. I hope I shall be in among the words, amazed at the controlled power of them; how they seem magnetized, held in tension above the ground. This is what I anticipate. And now I am going to read the poem.

Whilst I am reading a bird begins to sing loudly in the garden behind the house, and a car, or perhaps a bus, goes past under the railway bridge. I want very much to ignore these sounds, but hear them between the horizontal black and white bars and through the imagined sounding of the poem. My first reaction, on seeing the shape of the words on the pages, is something like "Ah, here it is!" – a bit like visiting a museum again years after one's first visit, and finding the same great sculpture in the very same spot. This poem is this poem, unmistakeably, not another one. The line break, the rupture in the tenth line, is very characteristic. The colon in the first line strikes me, "A sudden blow: the great wings beating still"; it is ugly, deliberately so, I think, and I'd forgotten it. The punctuation is radical. I am also impressed by word-combinations I'd forgotten; the thighs are caressed by "the dark webs". I'm a little dismayed this hadn't stuck. As I read on, I become more aware of the grandeur of the poem's sound, "And Agamemnon dead". Dead, as always, is heavily stressed, in my reading-head – I remember that. In the edition I'm reading (Macmillan's *The Poems of W.B. Yeats)* the poem runs across two pages, making a break between lines 11 and 12. This is annoying, and makes me think that (wherever possible) poems should always be printed on a single page. I am already forgetting, by the end of the sonnet, my response to the start – and I'm aware that I should be doing my best to remember. (I have a piece of paper ready to write my reaction down.) The word "blood" sticks out most of all: I follow a quick line of thought about Yeats and aristocracy and Lawrence and loins and cut it off before I get to Modernism and Fascism. I feel distracted and not enough in-the-poem; I've failed it. It's almost as if I haven't read the poem at all, just glanced it through: my eyes haven't entered the black of the words, they've just taken in that they are there on the page. Thinking back, I note how the confused grammar of the opening quatrain is followed by the rhetorical balance of the second; the Modernistic syntax of the next two and a half lines; the grand impending rise of the final three and a half. The "knowledge" to be put on makes me anxious: my own knowledge of the classics is inadequate to appreciate what exactly Yeats is alluding to. The poem seems so small for the presence it has in the literary world, yet it is so strong – a strong poem about overpowering strength, written, I note finally, in 1923.

LEDA AND THE SWAN

A sudden blow: the great wings beating still
Above the staggering girl, her thighs caressed
By the dark webs, her nape caught in his bill,
He holds her helpless breast upon his breast.

How can those terrified vague fingers push
The feathered glory from her loosening thighs?
And how can body, laid in that white rush,
But feel the strange heart beating where it lies?

A shudder in the loins engenders there
The broken wall, the burning roof and tower
And Agamemnon dead.

Being so caught up,
So mastered by the brute blood of the air,
Did she put on his knowledge with his power
Before the indifferent beak could let her drop?

What have I learnt from this? Not a great deal, really, but I have reminded myself of my earlier conviction that reading is a failure to read. Keats was aware of this. In his "little Region" "the images are so numerous that many are forgotten and found new in a second Reading: which may be food for a Week's stroll in the Summer?" This, for him, is the point of long poems, for readers "like this better than what they can read through before Mrs Williams comes down stairs". One of the best books about the failure of reading, and also its paradoxical success, is Nicholson Baker's *U&I*. Without re-reading any of John Updike's works, Baker analyses what from them has really been left in his memory; very little, it turns out, and that not very accurate. This is partly because Baker, like all of us, does not have a photocopying relationship to the text, and as Derrida has written about Joyce, even the idea of accurate quotation is highly problematic. Perhaps, following Philip Roth's great line from *American Pastoral*, the same goes for books as for people, for reading as for living: "The fact remains that getting people right is not what living is all about anyway. It's getting them wrong that is living, getting them wrong and wrong and wrong and then, on careful consideration, getting them wrong again."

The choice of "Leda and the Swan" for my experiment was not random. It is a poem about being overwhelmed, about being rendered powerless and through that, about gaining power, becoming a wielder of power. The idealised reading experience, the enchanted one, is not dissimilar to this: readers long to be overmastered, their will taken away (I just couldn't put it down). This is their fantasy. At the same time, as they spread the book open, *they* ravish *it* – take all it has to give them and then toss it, spine broken, aside. This, of course, is partly to recapitulate Yeats's gesture of making the male active, powerful, violent and the female passive, powerless and abused. It is also to argue that, this being objectionable, there may equally be something objectionable about reading. There is violence in the relationship, and it flows in both directions.

I'm aware, in all that I've written here, that the fact I am myself a writer perhaps distorts my reading to the extent that it is no longer even vaguely the same activity as for others. The argument of Harold Bloom's *The Anxiety of Influence* and *Map of Misreadings*, if followed and extended – which I think it can be – to novelists, would have it that I could do no other than distort Yeats – probably, though Bloom doesn't really go this far, misread my own misreadings as well as misreading my reading. For Bloom, I read in order to enter or continue an Oedipal struggle with the father-writer: I want to kill the book so that my own books can come to birth. There is, I think, a great deal of truth in this, and it is fairly rare that I feel myself to be reading without anxiety, without aggressively misreading. When I read a great writer, it's with a vengeance.

This is the first of two essays by Toby Litt. The second, "Writing", will appear in the Autumn issue of *Poetry Review.*

The Value of *Penniless Politics*

JOHN WILKINSON

A FEW EVENINGS ago I returned to my temporary Greenwich Village apartment and handsetted into C-SPAN, a cable broadcaster of wall-to-wall democratic process calculated to send the parish pump's greatest enthusiast scuttling to the trough for a cold and bracing douche of consumerism. My viewing served up a well-choreographed "demonstration" of Hispanic lobbyists protesting against a democrat filibuster delaying the nomination of the Republican Miguel Estrada to the US Court of Appeals (often a step towards the Supreme Court). The paraded stars alternated between silver-haired Southern state legislators, impeccably Anglo, disingenuously deploring the introduction of racial politics into the legal domain, while shamelessly schmoozing their Hispanic voting base; and Tex-Mex recording stars, several claiming long friendship with the Bush family and talking of their gratitude that in these times a great man leads the nation. "This great nation of ours" figured repeatedly, the other insistent trope being the embodiment in Miguel Estrada of the American Dream. The American Dream, in his progress via Columbia and Harvard Law School to the pinnacle of his profession, certainly trumps the reality of his actual, toxically conservative politics.

Witnessing this insulting farce, I was reminded of Douglas Oliver's poem *Penniless Politics*, first published in 1991 in London by Iain Sinclair, revised and reissued in 1994 by Bloodaxe in Newcastle. Betweentimes the poem made a print debut in New York (having been tested in public readings) as part of *The Scarlet Cabinet*, "a compendium of books" by Oliver and Alice Notley with, I imagine, a small readership. My fear is that *Penniless Politics* might come to be be neglected, despite unusual media attention for its 200-copy first edition, sparked by Howard Brenton's enthusiasm in the *Guardian*. (Brenton's piece is reprinted as a foreword to the Bloodaxe edition.)

Born on 14 September 1937 in Southampton and brought up in Bournemouth where Mary Shelley's body and Percy Bysshe Shelley's heart are buried, Douglas Oliver died in Paris on 21 April 2000 [1]. Much of his working life was spent in Paris, as a journalist working for Reuters and Agence France-Presse, and in the final period of his life teaching at the British Institute. He was always restive intellectually and persistently if considerately challenging.

As a poet, he was one of a kind; a kind which shook off any constituency as soon as it assembled. I would like to suggest what that odd kind of poet was, and could be for others; and how his poetics led Oliver, an Anglo-Scot who mocked his own plumminess, to write a narrative satire on US politics introducing (amidst various "non-poetic" matter) a draft for a revised US constitution. This poem must not be forgotten; whatever its poetic merit (if that can be separated from any other sort), it should engender disputatiousness beyond the confines of the poetry world. It is impossible to read *Penniless Politics* without thinking about what its extra-literary as well as literary consequences should be.

Poetry may be a lying art, but lyric poets often mean what they write when they write it. Douglas Oliver made sure he also *knew* about it, and was also interested in the way in which he and others knew: in the implications of knowing for action in both the private and public worlds. His poetic was concerned above all with what one might call pragmatic ethics. In lyric poetry, knowledge almost always stands subordinate to style and to affect:

and to exemplify how any of us might live personally and politically typically lies a long way off the lyric territory. Oliver's poetry, by contrast, was primarily an ethical project, perhaps uniquely in post-Romantic British poetry, and stylistically he employed whatever suited that purpose – or he turned to that purpose various of the writing styles developed by those close to him at different times. With his first book, *Oppo Hectic* (Ferry Press 1969) he was recognisably a "Cambridge poet" albeit a journalist passing through the city who found friendship and intellectual stimulus among poets he found there. This book and his first novel, *The Harmless Building* (1973) left recognisable traces behind in the poetry of Peter Riley for instance. But whereas in Riley "Trust", "Love" and "Kindness" were systematised within a philosophical framework derived from such writers as Merleau-Ponty and Heidegger, Oliver's ethics were much more rooted in his own experience, as the father of Tom, a child with Down's syndrome. This experience made possible an innocence beyond all the waddings of irony, a possibility of innocence responsible for the more remarkable passages of Oliver's poetry, including some in *Penniless Politics*.

Published in 1979 by the Ferry Press, *The Diagram Poems* looked as interestingly hermetic as a reader of the avant-garde might wish, its imposing format featuring, *en face* with the poems, elaborate doodles comprising circuits, cartoon animals, and the tracks of Tupamaros guerrilla operations. The poems were headed with brief prose narratives of guerrilla attacks on banks. This macaronic presentation had already been deployed in *In the Cave of Suicession* (Street Editions, 1974), a profoundly odd book of narrative, oracular dialogue and lyric poetry touch-typed in semi-darkness in a Derbyshire cave (hence orthographic errors such as that in the title) and discoursing with Tom, Oliver's dead son: the test that any ethics should be equal to an encounter with the death of one much-loved remained fundamental to Oliver's writing.

Oliver's introduction to *The Diagram Poems* plainly sets out this ethical ambition, as extended from its earlier, more personal, domain:

> But whether the guerrillas were right or wrong, you were dreaming quite obliquely, as you tapped the stories out, of how an authentic politics might combine the mildness of your dead baby with the stern wisdom of a judicious elder minister: some beneficial balance, instead of revolutionary flamboyance and a dictator's response of iron rule. Only a fool, while ill-informed, supports anyone else's violence . . .

That last comment is characteristic; Oliver may have been a liberal of an especially generous kind, but he was tough-minded, and *Penniless Politics* is filled with challenges to his own and others' too-lightly-acquired assumptions, enthusiasms, and purported experience.

At this point I wish to jump forward to *Penniless Politics*, vaulting across some of Oliver's most remarkable work (including the narrative poem denouncing Thatcherism, *The Infant and The Pearl* [2]). I began with a vignette of US political process as shown by C-SPAN; but yesterday evening (10 March, 2003) I turned to a local station to watch a city hall debate about the expected invasion of Iraq, overwhelmingly hostile to the war. During an interlude, one of those venerable pundits in whom American TV delights, was asked why the country was on the brink of war: "Why? Why?" he choked – "Because out of the South West dust a fanatic, a *fanatic* with *Jesus* in his eyes came to send boys from the Bronx to die, and said to Kids in Baghdad, on *their* birthdays it won't be candles on their cakes that get burnt, those kids will be set on fire and burnt by *our* missiles." His rage was so extreme and his age so advanced that I expected paramedics to rush into the studio. *Penniless Politics* registers simultaneously both the outrageously obvious corruption of American democracy, and also this rude, demotic energy and honesty – the residual but still-visible radical power more often encapsulated and neutralised in official ideology.

Oliver took that power as seriously as any right-wing militiaman does, with the crucial difference that his sense of the "Hooman", as he called it in *Penniless Politics*, exists in an intimate if constantly frictional relationship with diversity. He lived in New York City's Lower East Side from 1987 to 1992, as recounted in Alice Notley's excellent essay "Douglas Oliver's New York Poem" [3]. Notley does so impressive a job in summarising the complex plot of the poem that it makes any attempt of mine redundant, and she positions it exactly to its historical moment – closer to 1999 than to now, judging from her bemoaning of US politics' "lack of powerful symbols and of connection with scary forces. What if the President of the United States had to talk to the keeper of the Delphic Oracle from time to time [....] What if he had to face the gods before he decided policy?" Now we know.

But I must describe the poem briefly, with Notley's help. Supposedly written in *ottavo rima* derived from Tasso (although played very fast and loose) by a Francophile Brit living on the Lower East Side, the poem contains multitudes – a real New York poem in the Whitman tradition. Notley explains:

> The plot of the poem turns about the founding and progress of a new political party, called Spirit, without power or money. Invitations to the party's first meeting, instigated by Emen, a Haitian immigrant and Will, an Anglo-Scots immigrant, are by chain-letter. Crucial members of the party, the poem's characters, include Hispanic Dolores Esteves, a Cuban boxer named High John, African-American Ma Johnson, a young Korean woman (Republican) Yuhwa Lee, Juan her Hispanic boyfriend, the middle-aged Chinese man Peter Sung, the Jewish lawyer Lou Levinson.

The storyline of the poem recounts a version of urban regeneration which – improbably – benefits the residents of the area regenerated, and which is driven by fun, spectacle and a considerable amount of sex (in forms tending to mock existing power relations).

Brenton's foreword to the Bloodaxe edition notwithstanding, Oliver never set up the politically-engaged narrative poem as a standard for poetic conduct for himself or for others. Indeed this 'satire' works as a credible imaginary alternative to the sorry crack-blighted housing projects, the visible and miserably inhabited legacy of a policy of "benign neglect" and "planned shrinkage" brazenly articulated in 1970 by Nixon's advisor on urban policy, Daniel P. Moynihan, and implemented by successive City administrations; a policy of community destruction recently pursued by the sainted Rudy Giuliani.[4] Oliver's satire exposes such wicked folly not through denunciation primarily, but by producing a world we might wish at our best to inhabit, a world realised fully in its lusts, its zest, its quarrels, its errancy. Because we are so rarely at our best, that world never will be realised: but we are brought, nonetheless, to desire urgently to mobilise the spirit of Spirit in ourselves and for each other, and even – maybe – to promote some of Spirit's wholly pragmatic and sensible programme.

Oliver demonstrates beyond doubt that a postmodern poem can be stirringly political. What, after all, could be more "postmodern" than a voodoo spell kludged out of stanzas borrowed from Tasso's *Jerusalem Delivered* [5], and alive with the voices of half the world as mediated through their shared American experience? Oliver's poem vindicates the politics

and artistic practice of "diversity" – he relishes the linguistic, cultural and political encounters of Korean small capitalist with cool gay downtown lawyer with disillusioned turncoat Marxist journalist with Hispanic drugs-money launderer with African-American sporting icon. He likes the edges, the bumpy seams, not melange or gumbo. He acknowledges community as well as individual rights inasmuch as they conform to the "kind", the humane ("kind" being a crucial term for Oliver's writing). The powers of spirit and of lyric poetry expounded in *Penniless Politics* are founded in that romantic protest which was the historical forerunner of what some have termed "thick multiculturalism" and is based on a belief in the inexhaustibility of common human potential. The poem's new US Constitution derives from this romantic vision of diverse expressions of a shared spirit.

Strong narrative is necessary to a poem like this; unlike some other readers, I find Oliver's handling of formal rhymed stanzas insufficiently adept in itself to carry his arguments. Even within *Penniless Politics* the superiority of Oliver's free verse seems to me obvious in "Will's Incantation", both the most preposterous and the most deeply moving section of the poem. Its freedom, though, depends on the narrative and linguistic *milieu* already established:

> Oh Lord – Who is Lord? – Oh Lordess
> you are the bridegroom to Justess,
> which is female, a black mare of night,
> arise in your stable, Christess,
> in your groom's leather leggings arise:
> provide the stirrup that burns
> under the instep of the jockeys of night
> riding the black night mares
> shadows racing down the lost perspectives of street lamps
> past burning automobiles of darkness
> fires in the streets of lost civil rights
> the lanes of invisibles down lanes alternative to the fast lanes
> dearborn angel in black
> angel more than us arise from politics of contest
> not to end contest, but to add spurs and stirrups
> to the one, true race of our time.
> Come to this stable, Judaic Christess
> from your Italo-Irish Protestant cathedrals,
> take at last the white wafers of guilt from my mouth
> my tongue coated as if with thrush
> in my sorrow-song at those we have outlawed
> who die on the margins, in garishly-lit hospices
> or in African countries stricken with plague . . .

This passage exemplifies both how embarrassing Oliver can be in his innocence ("streets of lost civil rights"), and also the importance of such embarrassment. Oliver is unworried about looking foolish – this is part of his shtick, the white middle-aged male intellectual getting down on the dancefloor; the project for which the poem operates is too big for the poet's dignity to be material, and what the poem might animate is more important than its finished form. I must admit to having been one of the "middle-class well-educated whites", mentioned by Notley, who shrunk prissily (and in print, alas) from Oliver's willingness to make a spectacle of himself, failing to appreciate how closed, how exclusive, are the politics of standing on one's dignity. *Penniless Politics* is a stand-up act, taking pratfalls, sometimes awkward or routine, but whenever it hits its stride, the hits come thick and fast and thrilling.

Responsive then to the oral, semi-improvised poetics of contemporary New York, sure to gladden Shelley's heart in Bournemouth, reminiscent of Oliver's contemporary Barry MacSweeney (who died two weeks after him, and whose most moving writing was guided by the mute girl Pearl whom he taught to read, much as Oliver's was by Tom), this writing knows no shame in its pursuit of the good. Douglas Oliver was a good man, both unself-consciously and deliberately, and this is the first thing those who knew him say. I cannot think of another writer becoming a good person as an outgrowth of his or her project of writing or whose goodness so animated his writing. Whatever way this worked, it makes a lovely and more than ever required demand.

---

1. Two notable obituaries provide excellent summaries of Oliver's richly varied life, and of his literary work. Nicholas Johnson's for *The Times* has been made available on the website for the journal *Exquisite Corpse* [www.corpse.org/issue_5/burning_bush/ oliver.htm], while Andrew Crozier's for the *Guardian* with a further appreciation by Greg Chamberlain can be found online at www.guardian.co.uk/obituaries/story/0,3604,217852,00.html.

2. Two largely overlapping collections were issued, both including *The Infant and The Pearl* (Silver Hounds, for Ferry Press, 1985); *Kind* (Allardyce, Barnett, Publishers, 1987) and *Three Variations on the Theme of Harm* (Paladin, 1990). Both are unavailable. Currently available through internet booksellers is a *Selected Poems* published in the US by Talisman House (Jersey City, 1996). The author's Preface states: "These poems have been selected expressly to tell three linked stories at once. The first is autobiographical, the second political, and the third prosodic". Oddly these stories reduce the representation of *Penniless Politics* to the two free verse passages "White Crossroad" and "Will's Incantation". A memorial volume, *A Meeting for Douglas Oliver* was published in 2002 by three Cambridge presses, Infernal Methods, Street Editions and Poetical Histories, and includes 27 uncollected poems. In late 2003 Salt Publishing will issue a substantial volume of late and unpublished works titled *Arrondissements*. *Penniless Politics* remains in print from Bloodaxe.

3. This should be substituted for Brenton's in any reissue. Alice Notley, 'Douglas Oliver's New York Poem', *Chicago Review* v 45 no 1 (1999), pp79-88.

4. The best short account of this history lies in Deborah Wallace and Rodrick Wallace's pioneering work of urban ecology, *A Plague On Your Houses: How New York Was Burned Down and National Public Health Crumbled*, Verso, 1998. See especially Chapter 2.

5. Edward Fairfax's wonderful contemporary version published in 1600 (the original Italian was published in 1581) can be found in full at http://sunsite.berkeley.edu/OMACL/Tasso/.

Reviews

Giving Strawberries to a Dog

STEPHEN BURT

Christopher Logue, *All Day Permanent Red: War Music continued*

Faber, £8.99, ISBN 0571216862

CHRISTOPHER LOGUE BEGAN adapting the *Iliad* into modern English verse in 1959; unless you count Pound's "Propertius", few readers had seen anything like it. Logue took outrageous liberties, cutting and adding scenes, varying rhythms (a blank-verse base, short-lined inset lyrics, single ametrical lines), and retooling epic similes with deliberately modern material (rockets, radium, "Rommel after Alamein"). Logue spent twenty years on books 16-19 (the foray and death of Achilles' lover Patroclus; the fight over his corpse), then set to work on the Iliad's beginning, from the dispute between Achilles and Agamemnon that sets off the poem (*Kings*, 1991) to the duel between Menelaus and Paris, which might – but does not – prevent the rest of the war (*The Husbands*, 1994). These volumes brought Logue up through Homer's book four. They also brought him widespread, and deserved, adulation: the peculiar collaboration between Logue and Homer (and his mediators: Logue knows no Greek) captured both Homer's alienness and his contemporaneity; both his unstinting preoccupation with violence, and his ways of sketching character; both the religious background to the Iliad, in which gods and prayers make all the difference, and the concreteness of its descriptions, what Matthew Arnold famously called Homer's "eye on the object".

All Day Permanent Red adapts parts from books five through eight of the *Iliad*, the first books devoted at length to whole armies in combat; it contains Logue's first battle scenes in over twenty years, and it finds his powers of Homeric carnage undimmed. "The eyes of the crow and the eye of the camera open / Onto Homer's world, not ours", wrote W. H. Auden; Logue's best new passages (like many of his best older ones) draw on the eye of the (movie) camera, and on Logue's almost unparalled sense of pacing – when to speed a line up, when to slow down. The first page shows, ready for fighting, "the Ilian host/ Their coffin-topped rhinoceros and oxhide shields/ Packing the counter-slope". "The armies hum / As power-station outflow cables do." We see an arrow "carry a tunnel the width of a lipstick through Quist's neck". (Oddly-named minor characters – Quist, Gray, Chyláborrak, "Coriot and Shell" – are a minor Logue trademark; like the bizarre names in much science fiction, they establish that this book's world is not ours.) Later, unlucky soldiers "came away covered with blood and died / Like shoppers trapped by a calamity"; Hector's counterattack sprays "blood like a car-wash. / 'But it keeps the dust down.'" Clipped generalities provide variety, and bleak jokes: "The situation is unpromising"; "Not your day, Dio, not your day." Logue excels in snapshots, in epic similes, and in extended descriptions of physical action, driven by similes or by syntactic and phonetic mimesis:

> Extended lines of shields collide, totter apart
> Shuffle back shouting in their ankle dust
> Turning from lines to crescents, crescents to shorter lines
> Backstepping into circles or
> Parties just wandering about aimlessly....
> Headlock. Body slam. Hands that do not reach back. Low dust.

Homer's gods have little interest in human justice, nor in human constraints, though Homer's mortals persist in believing they do: Logue emphasises their arbitrary quality, at one (for him) with the arbitrary destructiveness – and the amoral thrill – of the violence humans inflict on one another. Odysseus prays to his patron goddess in diction befitting her station:

> As calm and cool as water in well.
> I know that you have cares enough
> Other than those of me and mine.
> Yet, Daughter of God, without your help
> We cannot last.

Athena responds, and Logue's diction reveals her real nature:

> Setting down her topaz saucer heaped with nectarine jelly
> Emptying her blood-red mouth set in her ice-white face
> Teenaged Athena jumped up and shrieked;
>   'Kill! Kill for me!
> Better to die than to live without killing!'
>
> Who says prayer does no good –

Heroes who pray more directly for success in slaughter generate cruder irony: "Blest Sister Wife of God / Give me the might and courage to become / The killer of the day." Ethics, rules, intimacy, constraints on appetite – all these projects belong, not to the gods, but to humankind, who, without these hard-to-achieve qualities, risk creating a world of nothing but war.

Logue's new volume imagines just such a world. "The noise they make while fighting", Logue-as-epic-narrator explains, "is so loud / That what you see is like a silent film." I was afraid to compare the volume to war movies until I found one reviewer had done so already: writing in *Slate*, Jim Lewis likens *Red* to the first reel of *Saving Private Ryan* – "everything has been elided but the fighting". Its limits resemble the limits of such filmmaking, the limits of merely sensory description: these heroes live in a spectacularly vivid sensory world, but in a very simplified – at times almost non-existent – psychological and emotional space. Real combat may produce just such effects (Logue, an ex-serviceman, might well know). Yet in earlier instalments of Logue's Homer, the warriors – even amid grotesquerie and carnage – could demonstrate motive and temperament. Hector had to balance his desire to defile Patroclus' body against his political judgment, which told him to keep the corpse intact (so he could trade it for Sarpedon's); Achilles' human grief, and his inhuman rage, came over whole from Homer's plot into Logue's words. In "Pax" (book 19) Logue explained "how / Men under discipline of death prepare for war":

> for a while they join a terrible equality;
> Are virtuous, self-sacrificing, free:
> And so insidious is this liberty
> That those surviving it will bear

An even greater servitude to its root:
Believing they were whole, while they were brave;
That they were rich, because their loot was great;
That war was meaningful, because they lost their friends.

And in *Kings* and *The Husbands* Logue put his sensory acuity to use in matters of character, matters of feeling. The sulking Achilles dismissed Greek messengers:

"Tell the commanders who may ask I meant my words.
I hate their King. He is a needle in my bread.
He is water. I am air. I honour you. Go.
Go."

Zeus (whom Logue calls – since Zeus is omnipotent – "God") ended a quarrel by telling his divine wife:

"You are the god of married love and of fertility.
So shut your mouth
Or I will kick the breath out of your bones."

And Hera did as she was told.

It was so quiet in Heaven that you could hear
The north wind pluck a chicken in Australia.

Later, Anchises told Hector the Greeks will never make peace:

"To them peace is a crime, and offers of diplomacy
Like giving strawberries to a dog.
Indeed, what sort of king excepting theirs
Would slit his daughter's throat to *start* a war?"

This new volume offers nothing like that.

Logue's Homer, as it continues to unfold, comprises not just a long collection of vivid lines, nor a neat interpretation of epic, but a project – a successful project – which aims to bring to contemporary poetry, using the resources proper to contemporary poetry, some of the drama, the vigour, the ethos and pathos long ceded to the novel and the feature film. Yet *All Day Permanent Red* has less in common with stage drama, or with the novel, than with a particularly hard-fought football match (one whose players routinely get spears through their eye-sockets). What *All Day Permanent Red* aims to do, it does well: readers who wish it did more – who wish it did what other books of Logue's Homer have done, dramatising distinguishable characters in an articulate epic frame – must simply wait. (Part of the problem lies arguably not with Logue but with the Homeric Diomedes, star of book five, who displays excellence on the field of arms, but not much of a personality off it.) Logue has promised that future books will "develop the contrast . . . between [Helen] and Andromache"; with luck, we will see not only those scenes, but also Homer's book nine – in some ways the core of the epic – in which articulate warriors and statesmen try to convince Achilles to rejoin their army, and he explains why he will not.

He Shoots, He Scores

STUART KELLY

Alec Finlay (Editorial Director), *The Pocketbooks Series*

16 volumes, Edinburgh, 1998-2002, £7.99 each

WHEN THE LATE Bob Cobbing, sound-poet and small press publisher, was called before his local Council for running a business from home (his Writers' Forum Press, which had produced nearly 1,200 items), the possible infraction was dismissed as "a hobby which had got out of hand". The publication of poetry can too often seem stranded between the extremes of the valiant enthusiast, reliant on persistence, modest visibility and aesthetic commitment, and the corporate behemoth, able to soak up losses from risky titles but always happier with a middle-brow, snazzily-packaged anthology of celebrities. This is a cliché, but, like most clichés, it contains an irritating grain of truth.

Alec Finlay's Pocketbooks series represented a different model for poetry publication. Not only did it boast high concept design and an avant-garde agenda, it achieved significant sales: indeed, several of the series have now sold out completely. Funded primarily though the Scottish Arts Council's National Lottery Fund, individual titles were co-published with bodies such as the National Galleries of Scotland, the DeMarco European Art Foundation, the Centre for Contemporary Arts, An Tuireann and Sadler's Wells.

Interdisciplinary, rather than vaguely multimedia, these books did not exist in a vacuum, but were the inspiration for, and record of, ongoing art projects, linking the visual arts, choreography, photography and critical reflection. They were catalogues of exhibitions as well as collections of writing; mementos of dance projects as well as hypothetical political provocations. This collaborative approach developed audiences for the work as much as participants in it. Between 1998 and 2002, the series produced sixteen titles, often including CDs, ranging from full length collections of poetry to anthologies exploring specific poetic forms, in addition to wholly visual works by David Shrigley, Helen Douglas, and Robin Gillanders. These "wordless texts" are not afterthoughts or asides, but intrinsic expressions of the aesthetics promoted throughout the series.

One of the earliest volumes (no. 2) was "Atoms of Delight: an anthology of Scottish haiku and short poems". Introduced by Kenneth White, the book contains examples of orthodox Japanese forms, senryu and renga as well as the frequently ill-treated haiku, counterpoised to "indigenous" Scottish miniature forms: proverbs, Ian Hamilton Finlay's one-word poems and Gael Turnbull's "Space" poems, in which, as he says, "something occurs between the first line and the last". Turnbull's eponymous "Space" exemplifies the unique property of his form:

> What might be said and then awaiting
>
> what has been said.

Throughout the book, the reader's focus is forced, even wrenched away from, the words on the page, into some absence outside the text. The anthology does not include one of White's own finest examples of this hazy dislocation between the poem's linguistic presence and absent denotation, "Snowy Moment in Montreal":

> Some poems have no title.
> This title has no poem,
> it's all out there.

There is a danger in such anthologies that the reader palls, that a surfeit of perfect *hors d'oeuvres* ruins the appetite. "Atoms of Delight" avoids this through judicious changes of register, accommodating bawdy humour, riddles and wry tipped winks. Alan Spence's Glasgow Zen pieces manage this through an internal "*para prosdokian*", or frustrated expectation between title and poem. For example, "On the implicit dualism of value judgements" leads to "IT'S AWFUL // GOOD". Similarly, Alexander Scott's definition poems work through the same disjunction: "Scotch Astrology // *Omen // In the gloamin.*"

"The Order of Things" (no. 10), extrapolated the brief mention of concrete haiku in "Atoms of Delight" into a full-blown consideration of "sound, pattern and concrete poems". With an assured sense of range and a generous editorial vision, Ken Cockburn and Alec Finlay produced a primer of forms: acrostics, toponymics, macaronics, and more. Again, there is an underlying concern with how poetry can decouple the conventional linguistic link between word and denotation. John Murray, in "Pool Poem", arranges the poacher's and angler's names, or nicknames, of salmon pools on the Teviot in the shape of the river. The poem "maps" the water, in much the same way as Edwin Morgan's "The Chaffinch Map of Scotland" constructs the recognisable, though significantly altered, land-mass out of specific dialect names for the bird.

"Unravelling the Ripple" (no. 13) and "Labanotation" (no. 16) pursue these interests to their conclusion. "Poetic" is an adjective normally used to describe anything except a poem, and in these two volumes the ramifications of using such a description are thoroughly excavated. "Unravelling the Ripple" comprises Helen Douglas's photographs of a Hebridean tideline, accompanied by Rebecca Solnit's essay. The crux is "tide-line": we are offered a wordless line, and asked to interpret it as a line of poetry, in terms of rhythms, caesuras, the cadence of shapes, and the enjambment between wrack and sand. Like the examples of concrete and minimalist poetics, it can be read as a sequence of metaphoric images, a set of representations, and simultaneously as "the thing itself".

"Labanotation", likewise, looks at the sports commentator's catchphrase acclamation "poetry in motion" in a new light. Archie Gemmill's World Cup goal (Scotland vs Holland, 1978) is transcribed into choreographical notation, and re-presented through professional dancers and schoolchildren's performances. Football Haiku (no. 15) collects the three-line haiku on paper that were printed as T-shirts for the Gemmill school workshops that ran at the same time, alongside the work of established poets. Alec Finlay's assertion that the pitch replaces the traditional pastoral associated with the form is as ingenious as it is dubious. In these volumes, much more than most, the book itself feels residual, a sloughed chrysalis of experience. Like a Goldsworthy photograph, the reader is unsure where exactly the phenomenon situates itself as "art": is it in the landscape, in the intervention, or in the "posthumous" recording of it?

The anthologies effectively made problematic many of the lazy definitions of poetry, dwindling the artefact down to a line, a hemistich, a single word; and expanding out into typographical cathedrals, alphabetic oceans, and walks across the Cairngorms – especially in Hamish Fulton's "Wild Life" (no. 6). "The Order of Things" closes, appropriately, with Tom Leonard's meditation on the differences between poetry and prose, where the most banal entries seem the most indisputable: "John Menzies doesn't stock poetry // whoever heard of war & peace having the line as the unit of semantic yield".

The series applied the same inclusive yet aesthetically selective approach to Scottish literary history. As mentioned above, poets like Kenneth White, Ian Hamilton Finlay and Gael Turnbull were, if not precisely highlighted, then certainly brought in to focus. All three pose problems for anthologists and critics, in that the "work" is often something beyond the page: a garden, like Little Sparta; an attitude towards the world, in White's geopoetics; a 'haptic interface', as in Gael Turnbull's *objets* (I mention in passing his poem written on a Möbius Strip, "Le loup du Pic Saint-Loup").

This less hierarchical approach to literary history culminated in "Justified Sinners" (no. 14), an "archaeology of Scottish counter-culture". In charting forty years of self-conscious avant-garde activity, from Beuys through to the K Foundation, it also drew attention to particular 'poetic' texts where the ostensible aim was not a beautiful arrangement on a page to divert a reader, but a piece of linguistic weaponry aimed at changing the world. The most obvious, and darkly wittiest, examples come from the Saint-Juste vigilantes, during Strathclyde Council's campaign against Hamilton Finlay's Little Sparta: "If he [the director General of the National Trust] won't have his head in his hands he can have his head in a basket." The curse, along with the prayer and the riddle, has, of course, been advanced as an origin for poetry.

In "Without Day" (no. 4) and "Wish I Was Here" (no. 5), this political agenda was as explicit, if less antagonistic. "Without Day" solicited proposals for a new Scottish parliament; it is the anthology as hypothetical assembly. The results are diverse, and there is a genuine strength in that diversity, even if some of the propositions err towards the kind of rowan and clarsach symbolism that one imagines would appeal all too much to public bodies. Those that run with the counterfactual kernel of the idea are better: Gavin Bowd's Houellebecq-esque fantasia on cloning, David Kinloch's study of thresholds and doorways, Bill Duncan's "Darkness Box" to ward off un-Calvinist levity (not for nothing is the technical term for love of gloom *scotophilia*).

"Wish I Was Here" considers multiculturalism. A "country" which is not a state imposes an implicitly vexed identity even on residents who can point to five generations of graves. Linguistically, the exploration of 'edginess' creates parallels between Gaelic and Urdu, Shetlandic and Arabic. Although the Scottish Poetry Library is emblazoned with the "Three Languages of Scotland" (Scots, Gaelic, and English) the anthology, without ghettoising, points to a richer and more subtly textured sense of linguistic inheritance and future development.

Pocketbooks showed how eminently collectable and intellectually provocative contemporary poetry could be produced through a combination of bold public funding and editorial panache. Many of the volumes are still available (in some galleries, and through internet book retailers): I would advise collecting them now, as their value, as well as their price, is sure to increase.

Mild Literary Necrophilia

JOHN REDMOND

Ian Duhig, *The Lammas Hireling*
Picador, £7.99, ISBN 0330492381

FINALLY, IN *The Lammas Hireling*, his fourth book, Ian Duhig has fulfilled the promise of *The Bradford Count*, his first. The skittishness which marred his second and third collections (*The Mersey Goldfish* and *Nominies*), and which gave rise to such flippancies as, "Sire, I am no soothsayer – to say other/ would be economical with the sooth", has receded. Although Duhig was never in much danger of taking himself too seriously, there remained a risk that he would not take himself seriously enough. He has held his poetry open – too open perhaps – to a variety of cultural sources – folk sayings, fairy-stories, urban mythologies, arcane etymologies, bits and bobs of high and low culture – and the effects, often, have been diffuse. Now, his focus has narrowed, his vision has deepened. He has produced a mature, concentrated work, emotionally centred, in a manner at once troubling and seductive, on what we might call "the liveliness of death".

We are alerted to this theme by the first line of the first poem, "Blood". The narrator, resplendent in his "oxblood oxfords", signals that he is wearing what was once alive. Thereafter, from poem to poem, we are obliged to reflect on the abattoir in the peignoir, on pelts and hides of every sort, from lederhosen and "cattel-skynne shoes" to "eggshell skin" and the "smelly old skin of an ox." There are, in addition, many references to what can be made of human or animal blood – some of them light ("I steal cows' blood in a bottle/ Because it fries up like a purple omelette") but extending, at their darkest, to what the Nazis made of the Grail myth. Repeatedly, corpses, or their products, serve to vivify the narrator ("I comforted myself recalling how the wild druids / Would get inside an ox-skin to see the future".) Pondering dead bodies is but another aspect of his fascination with cultural remains – words and phrases are themselves corpses to be skinned, themselves to be worn for show or protection. His concern with buried knowledge, with the fruitful interplay between imagination and secrecy, results in a mild literary necrophilia, suggests that nothing is more lively than that which has been exhumed. Living bodies, including his own, look unfinished or dull by comparison. In "Blood", for example, the narrator considers his untattooed form to be an "as-yet still-virginal unilluminated manuscript", his body not yet turned into a book. Adapting Mallarmé we might say that for Duhig the world exists to put into vellum.

Contrasting the animal-poems of Marianne Moore with those of D. H. Lawrence, R. P. Blackmur remarked how the latter made you feel that you had "touched the plasm" of the animal while the former made you feel something more abstract, less "live". One could produce a similar contrast by placing Duhig's animal-poems alongside those of Ted Hughes. Where Hughes ends his poem "An Otter" – the once-vibrant creature reduced to "this long pelt over the back of the chair" – is where Duhig, typically, would begin. The living in *The Lammas Hireling* are more abstract and ghostly than the dead. The body's live, animal "plasm" is subordinated to old idiosyncratic codes, of writing and custom.

At first glance, the cosmology of these poems seems very attractive: a world built on the magical principles of fairytales, vividly textured, with an almost medieval sense of interrelatedness:

When I told my son of Yu,
Born by Caesarean section
On the corpse of his father,
And of the virgins made pregnant
From stepping in God's footprints
Or from eating a swallow's egg,
He said, "Father, in past times,
Weren't there any natural births?"

For a while the poems make us feel that the anxieties and confusion of the modern may be held at bay, or even healed, if only we can remember what Njal called to Flosi across the Althing or how Columba proved that "the local sorcerer's bull's milk was really blood". Looked at more closely, however, one senses that the flip-side of this harmonious vision is extreme violence. The pain and anguish which these poems are reluctant to confront is deflected into curiously eroticised rituals, ceremonies of neatness:

I remember our true king pushing thorns through his penis,
Blood catching paper from which we priests read prophecies;
Now I see visions of a dragon-pale boy pushing a glass thorn
Into his penis, his last vein. For my King, this is law.

The influence of Michael Longley, which Duhig has identified as the major one on his poems, is evident throughout *The Lammas Hireling*: in the poems' syntax, pacing, framing of action and, to a certain degree, their outlook. Both Longley and Duhig are natural elegists. In "Rosary", for example, Duhig contemplates a meeting with the late poet Andrew Waterhouse:

He'll tell me again what he told me in the Bridge Hotel,
How the individual pages of the Lindisfarne Gospels,
If left too near a fire, shrink from it, and start
To reassume the shapes of calves they parted from
And I know if I ask, he'll tell me all their names.

One of the remaining drawbacks of Duhig's style is a slight sonic blur – but the depth and seriousness of this book more than compensate for such flaws. Like Longley, he writes poems which show a desire to comfort us. In his best work, like Longley, he overcomes this desire. In *The Lammas Hireling* he overcomes it as never before.

What's up, Doc?

SIMON COPPOCK

Wendy Mulford, *and suddenly, supposing: selected poems*
Etruscan, £9.50, ISBN 1901538427
Iain Sinclair, *Saddling the Rabbit*
Etruscan, £7.50, ISBN 1901538389

The moon
takes a taste of green
samplered
where waves stitch into the bay

THE MAINSTREAM NEGLECT of Wendy Mulford's "old explorations & unfinished endings" (to quote "once in fifty nights") is astonishing in light of this selection of her work from the late 1970s through the 1990s. While she is comfortable with the less tractable areas of visual/linguistic innovation (the second half of "Redheaded angels", for example, is a scatter of words, apparently culled from a medieval or Renaissance source text, thrown higgledy-piggledy across the page), the characteristic features of her work are lyrical clarity, impassioned and tender personal politics, and irreverent erudition. "Dampness smokes through / the art of loving are you / hard at work being modern", she asks in one poem from the excellent, elusive *Bay of Naples*, or in another poem later in the same sequence:

we
good-heartedly feature Latin America
'the most exciting continent'
our pain is / best / most personal / most
delicious no
one takes that from us

This restless, rapid movement between subjects and narrative positions runs through Mulford's work, even as poems dedicated to 1980s punks and post-punks give way to texts apparently appropriated from medieval women saints (about whom she has written a prose study) over the course of this broadly chronological selection. Yet for all that Mulford's poetry is postmodern in its play with syntax and semantics, it is her alchemical phrase-making that makes *and suddenly, supposing* a delight – "at dawn a path excludes nowhere / following a jungle / of white butterflies" ("Magi & oracle"), perhaps, or "the sea washes through like light" (*The East Anglia Sequence*). Of course, such isolated quotations give no sense of the cumulative power of her sequences of poems, among which *The ABC of Writing*, *The Bay of Naples*, and *The East Anglia Sequence* each merit a full review, as does the extended prose poem *La Pitie-Salpetriere* (published here for the first time).

The sequence gives Mulford the chance gently to turn over images and ideas in such a way as to explore their various contexts and interconnections, while gradually introducing the reader to particular descriptive techniques. *The ABC of Writing* offers a good example. In section c., she describes a reproduction oil-painting of a fishing-boat: "In the background, a dark-red/burnt sienna gaff-rigged? boat … A third man stands by the forward? mast, mending some thing, the boom and pulleys of the trawling net? Lobster creels? are on the deck, two with lids on. All these questions your boat gives me." The carefully gendered ignorance about fishing-boat terminology is simultaneously a joke about the empirical fastidiousness expected of the English poet; at the same time, the writing here is itself unusually fastidious in bothering to record the poet's apparent ignorance. In the glorious section **h.**, the question-mark fleetingly returns as a marker of the insufficiency of language as a means of transcribing natural beauty: "And the houses are Fishguard houses washed pale pink and blue with slate roofs; especially pink this evening in the gone-away-from-gold traces of blue-pink suffused in ? light – just light: off-cream off-pale-yellow off-white light and I cannot find its base." Then it takes a final bow in **i.**: "? to signify what *IS* requires an act of daily phenomenological daring in any order / and no little crudity", with the camp overstatement of "phenomenological daring" enhanced by the wry self-mockery of "no little crudity".

The way such techniques of collaboration with the reader are put to use by Mulford may be seen in "Elegy: Bradford, 1980". The poem initially seems bleakly (and properly) uncompromising

> The law says
> 'We cannot cater for every odd woman that gets murdered'
> and thirteen women die.
> Women say
> 'Curfew the men, let the streets be ours
> or let them die'

But for Mulford poetry is not a sledgehammer. Again there is the joke ("every odd [number] woman" / "thirteen women die"), which this time is in such bad taste that any sympathetic reader will try to ignore it. Yet once allowed, the joke leads into other areas of meaning: "odd woman" as madwoman, the woman who should be safe at home not out and about putting herself in danger. There are further turns in "Elegy":

> I am no protector.
> Through the open window the screech owl calls
> intimate human challenge.
> My arms around you are slight
> too slight for their task

and again:

> The violence waiting beneath the slates
> down in the derelict streets
> selects its chosen instruments
> to cuddle me

Both Mulford and Iain Sinclair began writing – and were distinguished editors – in the small-press scene of the 1970s. Both had poems included in *The New British Poetry* (1988), but Sinclair's star has since risen higher than Mulford's, in part due to his fiction and prose excursions, but also through wider publication of his poetry (*A Various Art,* 1987; *Flesh*

Eggs & Scalp Metal: Selected Poems 1970-1987, 1989; *Modern Poets 10*, with Denise Riley and Douglas Oliver, 1996). So while Etruscan should be praised simply for making such a healthy selection of Mulford's work available, the pocket-sized *Saddling the Rabbit* was always going to seem like a minor addition to Sinclair's *oeuvre*. It is nonetheless reassuringly "underground", in the '60s sense, with the one-line poem "Actor/producer Michael Douglas's definition of New York", for example, cocking a handful of snooks at stuffy cultural guardians (in full it reads:" 'somewhere between Los Angeles and Swansea' ") and the epigraph to "Continuous Sky" ("the artist's general disposition to vibrate") making Henry James sound like a blissed-out Wilhelm Reich. Sinclair's gift for compellingly mysterious titles is still in evidence: "Tassels, Bluebeards & Plaster Cheesecake", "The Slender Lozenge of the Eye", "Flesh is Hair Too".

A predilection for a kind of jump-cut surrealism is common to both Mulford and Sinclair, but for Sinclair it is often a shock tactic. The Imagistic "Telephone lavabo" (quoted here in full) is perhaps best described (in William S. Burroughs's phrase) as an "atrocious conceit":

> 3 pubic hairs
> in a cut porcelain egg
>
> piss stains
> on a chequered floor

This strangely fussy combination of the industrial-domestic with the grossly bodily shows Sinclair's close affinities with 1930s Surrealism. Indeed *Saddling the Rabbit* shares with the Surrealists a kind of troubled Romanticism, radical in tenor but fiercely individualist – notwithstanding Sinclair's gibe at "romantics who read French verse". The collection's prevailing theme is the erosion by top-down development of the working-class communities of London's East End. In "Letter to Prague", for example, Sinclair remarks "Spitalfields is so keen to echo its mythic past, sell tickets to tourist parties, property to aspirant New Georgians, that it has no time or energy to forge a contemporary existence". Earlier in the book ("Room Service Declined"), Sinclair mentions how a decaying house-synagogue, again in Spitalfields, attempts to emphasize particular government-friendly aspects of its history in order to secure funding to open as a museum; he calls this "The beginning of acceptable ignorance". Thus his writing is intended squarely as a defence of the arcane and marginalized against mainstream culture, a mainstream culture that is regarded as almost universally dreary.

Here there is a clear distinction between *Saddling* and *and suddenly*: Sinclair remains an "elective outsider" (to quote – out of context – his introduction to the exotically tendentious anthology *Conductors of Chaos* he edited for Paladin in 1996) because of society, whereas Mulford's struggle is to remain within despite society. In *The ABC of Writing*, after musing on the impossibility of buying escape from London's Isle of Dogs cheaply in the form of passage on a working boat from the East End docks, Mulford writes through her train of thought: "But it's not a far-off holiday I want, really. / What I want is knowledge. Inventing a destination would make no difference." This is not simply a matter of engagement. Indeed, Sinclair's poems here are more explicitly engaged with public politics – witness his moving "Reproduction Actors" ("it's too many years, deck boards & rivulets, since / I dreamt of a half-raised arm / the catastrophe on Brighton beach that did for / Old Labour, sodden kecks bringing out the small / boy in him, the once-&-never leader...") and the very funny account of New Labour's "summer 2002 neckware directive" in "Mr Moorcock is not Expected". Interestingly, Mulford (or perhaps her editor) have made a conscious decision to suppress some of the explicit political reference of her less-comprehensive small press selection of a decade ago (*Late Spring Next Year: Poems 1979-1985*): whether out of a sense that the political issues raised there (the Falklands War, Greenham Common protests) were no longer relevant, or from a belief that the poetry was improved without them. I certainly regret the absence of "Setting Sail for the Falkland Isles: Fools' Paradise". To return to *The ABC of Writing*, Mulford's description in section **h.** of how complex demands of motherhood affect female communication clearly stands for her poetics and politics also:

> That practice of being *available* ... *is* directive of *how* we listen ... fragmentation that by sleight-of-being stays whole for the audience at whatever cost to the performer: multiplicity that is not metonymic of privileged condition ...

By contrast there is a passivity about *Saddling the Rabbit*, for all Sinclair's linguistic fire-crackers: "Reproduction Actors", for example, ends "the tide / is feudally quiescent tonight, no economic migrants / the secret is out there and it doesn't change". Mulford indulges in the occasional bit of bohemian showboating, writing seductively that "for an artist time can always be regained / in the luxury of disarray" (in *Nevrazumitelny*), but she is too aware of the politics of domesticity to allow such fantasies too strong a hold:

> who am I to say
> do not who never could
> launder well
> a happy home
> ("Clean sheets", from *The Bay of Naples*)

Saddling the Rabbit is a bit of a rag-bag – prose oddments, a letter and poems – and as such inevitably suffers by comparison with the selected achievements of Mulford's career. Sinclair always digresses his way through his books, zig-zagging from prose to poetry, from squint-eyed empiricism to visionary disgust, but here the familiar hybrid feels too light, and Sinclair's linguistic magic-show seems all on-stage business and not much final trick. Mulford, on the other hand, proves herself a master of the anti-rhetorical flourish:

> hovers
> un-caught un-
> spoken the fellowship of
> repeats & thoughtful timidities
>
> ("At the bottom of the garden", from *The Bay of Naples*)

Etruscan books, tel: 01364 643 128. Cheques should be made out to Etruscan Books and sent to Nicholas Johnson, 28 Fowler's Court, Fore Street, Buckfastleigh, Devon EQ11 OAA. Postage: £1 for the first item, plus 50p for each additional item in the order.

Something for Nothing

WILLIAM WOOTTEN

Michael Hamburger, *From a Diary of Non-Events*

Anvil, £7.95, ISBN 0856463434

STARTING A DIARY in 1950, Michael Hamburger wrote: "There's so much that one can't put into one's poetry." Diaries, not Hamburger's early verse, made a fitting receptacle for what a poem of the time called "the wasted substance of our daily acts". Since then, Hamburger, who is an admirer of the poet, essayist and farmer Wendell Berry, has become a fierce opponent of contemporary wastefulness, and increasingly keen on making poetic use of the quotidian.

In *From a Diary of Non-Events*, diary and poem have become one. As the title suggests, if anything very exciting happened to Michael Hamburger between December 2000 and November 2001, he choose not to record it. Instead, it is the doings of plants, animals, and weather in Hamburger's garden and orchard and in the surrounding Suffolk countryside that the diary dwells upon. Nevertheless, events, including those of September 11, do intrude and prompt acerbic commentary on the wider world. Even local non-events start to tell the news. Indicators of climate change and foot and mouth are all about; and the prospect of genetically modified crops and animals gives Hamburger little hope for the future.

In such a bloody year for the British countryside, it is no surprise that a man who once dubbed some of his poems "owls' pellets" and who has used the alter-ego Mr Littlejoy doesn't take well to being told to "Look on the bright side!" by his neighbours. Nevertheless, the gloom can get overdone. To write in March of how "Intermissions of sunshine / dupe one daffodil into flower" is to give a true rendering of a false start to the season. To write in June of "Trees duped into their leafage" is to be ridiculous.

So the poetic diary is a fine sieve that catches, alongside little nuggets, some lines that might be better lost. More positively, the form often makes Hamburger's different modes intermingle and helps his registers and dictions to intertwine. The results can have a determined awkwardness – who else would write of "*a squirrel so deregulated*" or describe how a "belated black lamb, uncloned, / by a ewe, uncloned, is suckled"? – but they can also be arresting and pertinent. Hamburger presents garden and countryside, sometimes as correlative, sometimes as symptom, and sometimes as alternative to the political and ecological macrocosms. In so doing, he frequently essays a contemporary nature poetry that both registers and resists the effects that agri-industry, biotechnology and the consumer society are having upon the landscape and the language used to describe it. Thus, *From a Diary of Non-Events* can read less like the verse diary of a long-established author and more like notes towards a new, ecological, poetics.

But, however much one might admire Hamburger's sharp topicality and his assiduous commemoration of the day to day, it is those moments when he achieves something more timeless and rhapsodic that one most values:

> Wild honeysuckle it is that exhales a message
> To moths more sensed than seen,
> Evening primrose, weed, that answers with earthy brightness

A bat's wings now in the leavings of so much light,
The sky still limpid, starless
As though such effulgence had glutted
The need for luminaries far off, sterile as Mars.

Elsewhere, the succession of Hamburger's clauses can become a list of desultory observations. Here, however, inspired by deep breaths of wild honeysuckle, Hamburger makes his perceptions and syntax fluid, rather than disconnected, as he celebrates plant and animal life and the lingering effects of July light. The sentence may seem more logical if one decides that is moths not the message to them that are "more sensed than seen" by Michael Hamburger, but the suggestion that the poem is picking up signals from the natural world and its order, remains.

Something similar occurs when, in August, Hamburger celebrates the "Butterflies" pasture" of a "Tree-sized" buddleia: "The fragrant expanse of it, the summery hue / Massed on the level of bat's flight". Though Michael Hamburger has been a prolific and acclaimed translator, it is rare for his own poetry to evoke his translations, but such moments bring to mind lines from one of Hamburger's renderings of Paul Celan:

A tree-
high thought
tunes into light's pitch: there are
still songs to be sung on the other side
of mankind.

At his best, Michael Hamburger gives us an inkling of what those songs might be.

Forgotten Cities

PETER MANSON

Ciaran Carson, *Breaking News,*
The Gallery Press, £6.95, ISBN 1852353392
Justin Quinn, *Fuselage*
The Gallery Press, £6.95, ISBN 1852353295

CIARAN CARSON'S NEW collection *Breaking News* is a remarkable achievement of unity in contrast. From tiny, perfect poems like "Campaign" –

shot
the horse fell

a crow
plucked the eyes

time passed

from a socket
crept

a butterfly

– to the long sequence "The War Correspondent", which draws on the writing – often refunctioning the very words – of the Anglo-Irish journalist William Howard Russell, Carson displays a constant, playful inventiveness. Always he is discovering new ways in which the rhythms of spoken and written language (especially the journalistic) can come to be perceived as poetry. The influence of William Carlos Williams has been formative here. Carson's one explicit homage, "The Forgotten City", is a wry re-visioning of an Ulster which can sometimes seem as completely defined by The Troubles as Ancient Egypt is by its funerary practices. Williams's sense of pace, however, is everywhere in the book's shorter poems:

two men are
unloading beer

you can smell
the hops and yeast

the smouldering
heap of dung

just dropped by
one

of the great
blinkered drayhorses

("The Gladstone Bar circa 1954")

These effects – the peristaltic releasing of just a word or two at a time, and the line-break after an adjective in the penultimate line – both nod to Williams's red wheelbarrow or his "Poem" of 1930 ("As the cat / climbed over / the top of // the jamcloset / first the right / forefoot // carefully / then the hind / stepped down // into the pit of / the empty / flowerpot").

Carson's short poems mark small detonations in the surrounding silence, linked one to the other by recurrent imagery.

red alert
car parked

in a red
zone

about to

disintegrate
it's

oh

so quiet

you can
almost

hear it rust

("Breaking")

Here, Carson deftly inserts the pregnant pause into the poem itself, while making the poem participate in a series of contrasts between images of destruction by violence and through decay: old British Army regimental colours on display in St. Patrick's Cathedral, Dublin, "tattered by / the moth // or shot", the death in old age of a man whose life was saved when his pocket-watch stopped a bullet in the trenches. (This last image is itself linked to an account – presumably from Russell's journalism – of a soldier saved when a bullet "stopped / at Revelation" in his pocket bible).

The vision of Belfast as a place crippled by mutual surveillance — where the sudden withdrawal of an army helicopter can make the poet feel as if rinsed clean, where he can awaken to the sound of a bomb-blast ("near dawn // boom // the window / trembled // bomb // I thought") but still notice the untroubled emblematic blackbird whistling in the silence that follows – forms a counterpoint to the often astonishing poetry Carson draws out of Russell's despatches from the Crimean War. Carson gives us casual beheadings by artillery fire, the reduction of people – and above all horses – to tatters of cloth and bone, and an account which perceives the great fire which destroyed a quarter of the town of Varna largely in terms of its inconvenience to the allied forces:

both the French and we were dispossessed
of immense quantities of goods –

barrels of biscuits, nails, butter, and bullets,
carpenters' tool-boxes, hat-boxes, cages of live pullets,
polo-sticks, Lord Raglan's portable library of books,
and 19,000 pairs of soldiers' boots

The accumulation of such details, and the understated compassion and anger which Carson discovers in them, places "The War Correspondent", and *Breaking News* as a whole, firmly in the tradition of such great twentieth-century acts of recovery as Charles Reznikoff's *Testimony*.

Justin Quinn's *Fuselage* is a much more difficult book to approach. Quinn was born in Dublin, but now lives and works in Prague, and I wonder how much the experience of living among the speakers of another language has influenced the oddly inward quality of his verse. If it's sometimes hard to know who, or what, is being addressed in these poems, their often Mallarméan sinuousness intrigues, and rewards repeated reading:

The surface coils and rends
itself so monstrously –

swirls flicker strenuously,
then sink like sodden fronds,

as though beneath the surface
something huge had woken –
lazy, moving, limber –

for seconds, and now swerves
off sideways and back down
again into light slumber.

Quinn is not always as oblique as this, but a lingering mystery still attaches to the most straightforwardly-phrased of these poems, heightened by the sense that the poems' dialogue is at least as much with the structure of their own verse-forms (loosely iambic, usually rhymed) as with any clearly-imagined interlocutor. Any suspicion that rhyme might be driving the poems beyond Quinn's control tends to dissipate when the book is considered as a whole. In a poem on the poet's house in Prague, the house

seems
to slightly float, to flow, to give and tilt
within the greater tilt and give and flow
of Prague at large through black and gold and red –
so many millions packed into its felloe
and swung through centuries, so many dead
who added facets to the ebb and flash
and faded into what they came from: ash.

The twist in the last line, where people return to ash rather than the canonical dust, seems strange until the reader comes to the subsequent poem's mention of the self-immolation of Jan Palach, and realises one sense in which the modern Czech Republic was indeed founded on ashes.

The poems of *Fuselage* often work like this, building into larger structures like the sequence on sleep and awakening near the opening of the book, which bears comparison with those moments in *Finnegans Wake* when the dream-state lifts to reveal hints of the dreamer's physical surroundings. I don't want to over-stress the book's complexities, as it contains a good deal of poetry that communicates at first encounter, such as a sequence about a visit to London to meet old friends ("And, Jesus, get me out of here, / I think as I step on the shuttle"), or this entertaining line in consumerist irritation:

so that when you lift your hand out through the space,
the very air, of the supermarket that's faceted with choice

you'll feel that this product is for you,
that your personality is best expressed

through its purchase; it's you; you know it too
and ferry it home with the kind of consumer pride

> you associate with the 1940s and '50s
> when the world was a better place, and Ma
>
> was not your Da in drag (like now)

This perspective, too, becomes darker and more complex as the book proceeds (and note in passing that Quinn's poetry is as difficult to quote from as Carson's, carefully-managed long syntax often sustaining a single sentence to the length of a page). *Fuselage* is an important, rewarding, often baffling collection, a book I look forward to living with.

Crash Course

JOHN MCAULIFFE

Jamie McKendrick, *Ink Stone*

Faber, £8.99, ISBN 0571215327

Lachlann Mackinnon, *The Jupiter Collisions*

Faber, £8.99, ISBN 0571216552

WILLIAM BLAKE'S "INTRODUCTION" to *Songs of Innocence* provides an unlikely epigraph to Jamie McKendrick's *Ink Stone*. The simplicity of Blake's "And I made a rural pen, / And I stain'd the water clear" could hardly be further removed from "Apotheosis", the collection's first poem, which starts off like a parody of Tom Paulin "His bonce high-domed like a skep, the bee-man / holds forth". The poem, a sonnet, revolves around this man with a bee in his bonnet who, of course, "won't [loosen] his hold on the bee one micro-notch" and so streaks out of a window. The sestet's seemingly gratuitous reference to a "micro-notch" calls attention to the most interesting and enjoyable aspect of the collection. Although *Ink Stone* contains numerous light and ephemeral notes on houses, neighbours, travel, food, and the latest in the long jam of McKendrick cars (four years of Citroen driving now), the poems are, typically, full of ore-loaded, confected, allusive, and playful filler. In the book's second poem,"Bee Line", for instance, the first verse exists purely for its glut of gs:

> The novice keepers, togged in gloves and goggles,
> smoked out the spirit of the hive and laid
> three trays, each caked with hexagons,
> on the oak table where they sat and ogled
> the gold light trapped in the grid of cells
> till their lids grew heavy and they trudged to bed.

When this relishable style – packed with ornamental detail and consonantal cymbal clashes – meets inspired subject matter, which happens most enviably and consistently in the translations of Rilke, Lorca, Montale and Brecht, the effect is explosive. These McKendrized foreigners buzz with strangeness and life.

In his own poems there is often an enjoyable dandyishness to his self-representation, though this can undercut the work's actual qualities. And sometimes, it must be said, the poems are not so much undercut as sabotaged by the arch but overly predictable comedy of his encounters with the world. He seems, however, to find ways into strangeness and fantasy – and out of mere whimsy – in the translations and in the poems where he avoids travel or simple exercises in social persona. In "Sea Salt", for instance, he writes a sonnet version of Yeats's "Politics": but where Yeats's head is turned from politics by desire, McKendrick turns from desire to the sort of detail and weird accumulation of sounds in which he specialises: witness "a crystal / she'd shed from the salt bowl" which then mutates into, among other things, "the kind of roof a child might put / on a painted house" and "a see-through pyramid". "Beyond" does more with his gift for phrasing, combining it more affectingly with his participant-observer persona. The poem begins by reporting, just a little fussily, on the reactions of an accident victim – "(it seems a choice / was offered him)" – before zoning in on the pain, "an entire horizon of hot wire," and then striking the poem's disbelievingly elegiac note, "I told him about your accident, Lee, / the speed you were going, not forty miles per hour" and later, as if from miles away, describes the "fateful shiny insect torso of the bike". There is a lovely echo, too, of the Blake epigraph in "Beyond", with its reference to the "moment that has stained our lives".

Ink Stone begins with a buzz and there is a humming originality and strangeness to its best poems. Whatever happened, though, to the Dante translation at the end? Its six pages are easily the least interesting poem in the book, ending all too predictably by disappearing "without a trace".

Jamie McKendrick and Lachlann Mackinnon's collections share an allusive sensibility but little else. While McKendrick usually packs his line and uses its regularity to explore the words and stretch out the themes he addresses, Mackinnon's *The Jupiter Collisions* seems more attentive to the turn of the line and in the turn's first impact on the reader. The title poem offers an example on an unusually grand scale: the poet connects a personal experience, a couple walking by a river, to an exceedingly unlikely parallel, a comet disintegrating in Jupiter's gravitational pull. The "collision" of perspectives in this poem also occurs in the more philosophical sequences, "Pips in a Watermelon" and "A Water-Buffalo in Guangdong Province", where Mackinnon floats an idea and then seizes on a particular detail to bring it to life so that "Can I perceive an object / that isn't here?" is counterpointed with "The hard nipples of a boy / in a changing room"; "The world is not a poem / though it was made" with "A burger box rattles and blows about ajar"; and "heaven is carnal" with "brought /earwax and semen / to the tip of the tongue". These conceits at first seem metaphysical but, in their dissociatedness and in spite of the intelligence and interest of the connections, they also call to mind the kind of experimental poetry that juxtaposes disparate idioms, forcing transitions which the reader registers rather than credits.

Music is notoriously unrewarding to write about and Mackinnon bravely attempts tributes to Jerry Garcia, Bob Dylan and the Beatles, but the poems clarify the difficulties of Mackinnon's style. All three poems resort to traditional perspectives on art to isolate and canonise their rock'n'roll subjects: in the very short "Not Fade Away", Garcia is imagined as an organic creator whose early and late records fade into one another and Dylan, unfortunately, is reduced to a biographical cartoon (Minnesota, James Dean, harmonica and Baudelaire). It is as if deprived of the energy of collision or juxtaposition the poems lack detail or depth. The *Beatles* tribute remembers their London rooftop gig but alludes all too predictably to the clichés of "Get Back", the "times are changing" and their "last great single". Each of the two stanzas includes the phrase, "nobody knows this", but Mackinnon fails to generate a sense of three-dimensional occasion about the too-well-known iconic image. His elegies for writers, too, evince a dutifulness even as they enthuse about their

cati del mondo, abbi pietà di noi; **tu che togli i peccati del mondo, accogli la nostra supplica**; tu che siedi alla destra del Padre, abbi pietà di noi. **Perché tu solo il Santo**, tu solo il Signore, **tu solo l'Altissimo, Gesù Cristo, con lo Spirito Santo**: nella gloria di Dio Padre. **Amen.**

COLLETTA - O Dio, che hai preparato beni invisibili per coloro che ti amano, [illegible] la dolcezza del tuo amore, perché amandoti in ogni cosa e sopra ogni cosa, otteniamo i beni da te promessi, che superano ogni desiderio. Per il nostro Signore... **A - Amen.**

Oppure la colletta Anno A, dal Messale, pag. [illegible]

C - O Padre, che nell'accondiscendenza del tuo Figlio mite e umile di cuore hai compiuto il disegno universale di salvezza, rivestici dei suoi sentimenti, perché rendiamo continua testimonianza con le parole e con le opere al tuo amore eterno e fedele. Per il nostro Signore Gesù Cristo, tuo Figlio... **A - Amen.**

LITURGIA DELLA PAROLA

PRIMA LETTURA seduti

Il brano del "terzo Isaia" riporta un oracolo che parla di un ingresso di stranieri nel popolo eletto: «Il tempio di Dio sarà casa di preghiera per tutti i popoli».

Dal libro del profeta Isaia (56,1.6-7)

[1]Così dice il Signore: «Osservate il diritto e praticate la giustizia, perché prossima a venire è la mia salvezza, la mia giustizia sta per rivelarsi. [6]Gli stranieri, che hanno aderito al Signore per servirlo e per amare il nome del Signore, e per essere suoi servi, quanti si guardano dal profanare il sabato e restano fermi nella mia alleanza, [7]li condurrò sul mio monte santo e li colmerò di gioia nella mia casa di preghiera. I loro olocausti e i loro sacrifici saranno graditi sul mio altare, perché il mio tempio si chiamerà casa di preghiera per tutti i popoli».

Parola di Dio. **A - Rendiamo grazie a Dio.**

SALMO RESPONSORIALE (Salmo 66,2-3.5-6.8)

Ringraziamo il Signore perché ha voluto che il suo disegno di salvezza fosse esteso a tutti i popoli. Per questo con il salmista diciamo (o cantiamo):

Rit. **Popoli tutti, lodate il Signore.**

Po - po - li [illegible] gno - re [illegible] lu [illegible] ia!

Oppure: **Popoli tutti, lodate il Signore, alleluia.**

Dio abbia pietà di noi e ci benedica, / su di noi faccia splendere il suo volto; / perché si conosca sulla terra la tua via, / fra tutte le genti la tua salvezza. Rit.

Esultino le genti e si rallegrino, / perché giudichi i popoli con giustizia, / governi le nazioni sulla terra. Rit.

Ti lodino i popoli, Dio, / ti lodino i popoli tutti. / Ci benedica Dio e lo temano tutti i confini della terra. Rit.

SECONDA LETTURA

La promessa di Dio è irrevocabile. Il popolo d'Israele rimane l'eletto, ma il suo rifiuto è diventato occasione di grazia per i pagani.

Dalla lettera di san Paolo apostolo ai Romani (11,13-15.29-32)

[13]Fratelli, ecco che cosa dico a voi, Gentili: come apostolo dei Gentili, io faccio onore al mio ministero, [14]nella speranza di suscitare la gelosia di quelli del mio sangue e di salvarne alcuni. [15]Se infatti il loro rifiuto ha segnato la riconciliazione del mondo, quale potrà mai essere la loro riammissione, se non una risurrezione dai morti? [29]Perché i doni e la chiamata di Dio sono irrevocabili!

[30]Come voi un tempo siete stati disobbedienti a Dio e ora avete ottenuto misericordia a motivo della loro disobbedienza, [31]così anch'essi ora sono diventati disobbedienti in vista della misericordia usata verso di voi, perché anch'essi ottengano misericordia. [32]Dio infatti ha rinchiuso tutti nella disobbedienza, per usare a tutti misericordia!

Parola di Dio. **A - Rendiamo grazie a Dio.**

CANTO AL VANGELO (Cf. Matteo 4,23) in piedi

Rit. **Alleluia, alleluia.**

Gesù predicava la buona novella del regno e curava ogni sorta di infermità nel popolo.

Alleluia.

VANGELO

L'atteggiamento della cananèa è esemplare per descrivere la fede: riconoscere di avere bisogno della salvezza senza averne il diritto, e accogliere la misericordia di Colui che ci ama.

Dal vangelo secondo Matteo (15,21-28)

A - Gloria a te, o Signore.

In quel tempo, [21]partito di là, Gesù si diresse verso le parti di Tiro e Sidóne. [22]Ed ecco una donna cananèa, che veniva da quelle regioni, si mise a gridare: «Pietà di me, Signore, figlio di Davide. Mia figlia è crudelmente tormentata da un demonio». [23]Ma egli non le rivolse neppure una parola. Allora i discepoli gli si accostarono implorando: «Esaudiscila, vedi come

12 TEMPO ORDINARIO

DAVID GODBOLD

Roma 20/08/12

DEAR RESIDENTS,
PURCHASED BY THE SCHOLARS FOR THEIR
OWN USE.
THANKS FOR YOUR CO-OPERATION.
DAVID ★ GODBOLD
The capacity for
differentiation between past, present
and future
is clearly important.
8/07/02
'Roman Orator'

Eh! Egh! Murder! Murder! *etc*.
DAVID
GODBOLD

Tough
DAVID GODBOLD
We all dream of living amongst
thoughtful and caring people
1/8/02
Rome

subjects: daubed-on adjectives do a lot of work. We read, for instance, about "The good poet William Stafford" or about "sad Ezra Pound", who is imagined, despite the continuing vigour of his prosodic experiments and the never-ending debates about his politics, "rapt from time like a verse sealed in itself by form". The collection ends where it began, but doubting its own imagined meanings: again, a couple walks by a river, aware of their place in the universal scheme of things, but still in search of significance: "perhaps our lives, tiny as they may be, are added / to a vast chorus that roars in the ears of God."

Hopping Down the Great Gallery

JANE GRIFFITHS

Peter Scupham, *Collected Poems*,

Oxford/Carcanet, £14.95, ISBN1903039576

PETER SCUPHAM'S *Collected Poems* is truly a *Collected*, bringing together all his books from the early and rare *The Small Containers* and *The Snowing Globe* (1972) to his most recent *Night Watch* (1999). While it has been Scupham's practice to give each volume a central theme, the gathering of all his works reveals how strongly interconnected these themes are. It shows an imagination playing constantly around a cluster of related images, but also a quite startling change of focus in his treatment of them.

Scupham is consistently drawn to what is evanescent: a child's puppet show, a paper Christmas lantern none the less talismanic for being "Such flim-flam: a hutch of crumbling card / And the light's composure" and, repeatedly, the theatre. In the final poem in the volume, "This Late Tempest", a second Prospero's address to his Ariel concludes not with benediction and dismissal but with the summons to a repeat performance:

> There – thunder at the sea's sharp rim.
> And all begin again.
>
> "Approach, my Ariel, come!"

This beginning again is both effort and renewal. The action on stage becomes the equivalent of the four chalked fish of an early poem, which swim colourfully on a dark ground until "Knowing our task is / To feed the invisible with our images, / We rub the blackboard clear".

In his early writing, Scupham's sprezzatura is perhaps most obvious in the title-sequence of *The Hinterland*, a series of fifteen linked sonnets in which each last line becomes the first line of the following sonnet, and the fifteenth sonnet consists entirely of these repeated lines. The main subject of the poem is the lost generation of World War I, so that the sonnet-form has a historical appropriateness – the poet's call on the goddess echo, as Scupham puts it elsewhere. But just as the poem is more than an elegy for a past generation, so too the form is more than pastiche. In its juxtaposition of Edwardian and wartime summers with the 1970s summer when "the shagged elms tower and die", the sequence reveals far more than the ability to make an equation come out. Rather, its repetitions play the cyclical against the momentary and particular, and suggest that there is no safe and certain boundary between the two.

In Scupham's later work, formal structure remains important as a means of imposing momentary order on chaos, but here too there is a constant awareness of the fragility of its arrangements. In *The Air Show*, turning directly to his childhood, Scupham is almost overwhelmed by the richly remembered detail:

> The tree loaded with plums, its sage-green fingers
> Knuckled on purples, mottles, bobbles of gum,
> The pale snail-shells footing the garden wall.
> The brass plate by the door at the end of the drive
> Polishes itself away summer by summer.

As in *The Hinterland* and *Prehistories*, Scupham is caught between a sense of permanence and a knowledge of impermanence, but where the earlier works seek for a solution in a shared identity, here there is a tremendous tension between private and public history. The title poem, "The Air Show", depends on this discrepancy to image war and the rumour of war during the 1930s as a "buzz of flies and voices"; it shows precisely how, to the child, his childhood is inviolable, but tilts against that security its own knowledge of his place in history:

> A tri-plane bellies its fabric into the sunshine
>
> ...
>
> ... High overhead,
> The little silver gnats tow rolling banners
> Lettered with huge but cryptic messages.
> The sky is very open, very endless,
> And lying on my back with my head cupped
> I feel the world go twirling softly round
> Like an old waltz.

Elsewhere, this imbalance is brought still more sharply into focus by direct reference to the worst of the war, grasping the almost impossible subject of the holocaust by concentrating on what was known to the child at the time. There is the little Spanish train that curls in the hand and turns itself seamlessly, allusively into the transport to Auschwitz, even as it remains "a wooden train / Quite serious in its unclouded paintwork, / Its yellow bright as any Star of David". There are the German bricks, "boxed up tight / With all their paper citizens", so that even at the end of the night

> ... not a column, brick or spire is lost;
> The picture still confirms it: none is lost.
> Where Jacob Schutz sheltered, a child cried endlessly
> Jesus, my Jesus, Mercy, Mercy.

These are astonishing poems, enacting containment just as the German bricks do, yet constantly bringing into question just how sustainable such containment is.

This is a question which continues to haunt Scupham's subsequent work. In "Accident", which can only be described as an anti-sonnet-sequence, he addresses it directly. Just as the putative victims of a road accident are stripped of all their qualifying adjectives, sent home for dinner, reduced to scribbles on the page and figures in "a rotten likeness of something" up for auction, all in a sequence of loosely scanned and largely unrhymed fourteen-liners, the poem turns on the very idea of formality in purposely trite scansion and rhyme:

> *I'm telling you the truth.* Because we *share*
> ...
> It is important that we learn to trust,
> If not each other, girl and road and man.
> Do not believe the useful rhyme of "dust".

This has the air of Edward Lear giggling furibundiously and hopping on one leg down the great gallery, yet it also raises serious questions about the way in which poetry of necessity reinvents things on its own terms. Increasingly, in Scupham's later work, there is an attempt not to invent but to leave be; the long elegy for his father is cast almost wholly in his father's own words. These are frequently humorous ("... if you see a book that's not worth reading, / Pass it to me, and I won't read it"), and just as often disconcerting, as in "Who do you say you are?", which opens with the question: "Life's difficult. How do you know you're not me?" and concludes:

> "You know too much.
> You claim you're Peter?
> There are certain sorts of knowledge that are forbidden
> And there's only one source they can come from,
> And that's the Devil.
>
> Are you the Devil?"

In these poems, apparently almost unedited records of direct speech, the fact of the matter is allowed its own unmediated weight. Just as the poet's mother in "Young Ghost" is photographed and so is "safe ... from dying with what is dying", so his father here is preserved in snapshot form, as he was. Yet this too is (in the words of "Accident") "A coarse and grainy stuff that's not explained / By titling it in bold '**Life**', '**Memory**'". Rather, the idea of a life becomes, like the fact of a poem or the house in "The Provisional Thing", apparent solids to set against the wind which sings "for the space, provisional, / The house is in default of". Whether in a display of dazzling technical virtuosity or in the open-ended forms of much of his later writing, Scupham's poems persist, movingly, in shaping images to feed the invisible.

Salt Beef

RICHARD PRICE

Geoffrey O'Brien, *A View of Buildings and Water*
Salt, £8.95, ISBN 1876857552
Brian Henry, *American Incident*
Salt, £9.95, ISBN 1876857528
Andrew Grace, *A Belonging Field*
Salt, £8.95, ISBN 1876857455
Nicholas Johnson, *Cleave*
Etruscan, £6.50, ISBN 1901538451

All the same
it's better to weigh your words
before remaining silent

AT ITS BEST, Geoffrey O'Brien's *A View of Buildings and Water* is witty and pleasurably wrong-footing, like these three lines of his, an imagism-of-the-mind, perhaps, which draws comparison with Frank Kuppner's amusing chinoiserie. I think I hear Wallace Steven's blackbird variations in the longish piece "The Lake", in which "All morning the furrows / repeat nothing". It's in his landscapes, however, that I like O'Brien best: he seems over-sketchy and unfocused in his urban poems, but his landscapes are attentive, and can be oddly claustrophobic, even intimate. I especially liked a little reference in one poem to glasses dropping down the nose, a reminder of both the mediation and interrupted concentration in O'Brien's act of seeing. With the short lines of his big outdoors poems I presume the convention of a slow pace, a reflectiveness that is one of reading's great pleasures, even if a headlong kerfuffle is another.

Like the other two American Salt-published authors under review here, O'Brien employs titles which betray a nostalgia for, or craftmanslike remembrance of, old forms and styles: "Sonic Ode", "Songs Done In Praise of Winter", "Late Geometric Grave-Offering". Actually, despite one or two dust-jacket testimonials that hint at the contrary, there is no sense, in any of these authors' work, that these poets are pushing word by word, line by line – and title by title – into a refreshed poetic language; only Brian Henry appears to harbour that ambition, and even he interprets it in a distancing, know-it-all way, rather than having his poems manifest it in their actual substance. There is something a little academic, too, about what I take to be O'Brien's engagement with Frazer's *Golden Bough* in one poem ("Sonic Ode"), but he laughs back at me with these lines:

It was never clear if the hole
In the lower right corner of the stanza
Was the remnant of a tomb door
Or the path to the picnic area.

Brian Henry's *American Incident* is more mannered than O'Brien's work, with a predeliction for some rather arch language which, despite the recurring Crime Scene Investigation theme (prose pieces in a fragment collection called "Patricide in C Minor"), can be closer to a polite academic paper than a detective procedural. If lines like "Imagine, if you will, dying / by scratching" are lines from the street, it's a pedestrianised one, "if you will", on campus. His work also shares something with the gothic absurd that W. N. Herbert brought over from comics. There is a confident, assertive prosody, though, and that's worth sticking with. Literature and its schools is a key subject, even more than for O'Brien: there are meditations here on Shakespeare, and on the nature of realism, and poems entitled "Naturalism, or In the Cathedral of Decadence", and "Content". I like Henry best when he is not ruminating on the big exam questions of Literature, as in this deliberately all-fingers-and-thumbs end to "Lap Toy":

> Spittle and hugs for lips. Around jeans the envy closes.

In this example, the wit approaches that of Harryette Mullen's prose poems, and here Henry's fondness for abstract nouns starts to zip itself up, for the better. Elsewhere the poems are marred by a disappointing lack of visuality and in a book of over one hundred and fifty pages, perhaps more editorial negotiation was required to let more lines like this one breathe.

The permutations in George W. Bush's language that Henry uses in the way that Donald Rumsfeld's words have been more recently used (see **www.slate.msn.com/id/2081042**) offer an unexpectedly precise focus – a real unabstracted target, here – and a welcome if early prosodic break. As with the Rumsfeld satire, there is maybe an assumption in such re-appropriation that these powerful men do not understand the language they are using: that they are clowns. I think such an assumption, if that is the assumption, is incorrect: Bush and Rumsfeld make another kind of sense, even another kind of poetry, in their use of a homely but powdered soup of colloquialism and policy-speak. This is one of the areas where the English language is growing, however repugnant the meanings beneath their statements are: perhaps this language is available for other than authoritarian and, by the same token, satiric purposes?

Andrew Grace's *A Belonging Field* is a book of great promise. I know there's a gerundic cliché in the title. There's also something which has become a tic in contemporary poetry: an educational discipline or concept yoked to a natural phenomenon or psychological state – in other poets' work a "history" of this, "architectures" of that, "cartographies" here and there of who knows what – and Grace has quite a few of those: "underlord of desperate mathematics" ("Gnats") for example. But this exquisite book, which is largely about childhood in what I guess is the Mid-west, also has: "A seed-bag impaled on the rooster's / iron mohawk waved the flag of a barn's bankrupted roof" ("Hail") and "My room's warmth is like that trapped between two mouths" ("Flies"). I don't quite trust my own judgement when poets are precise with the botanical and folk names of plants and flowers – they're easy litanies, but seduction by litany is OK by me – and Grace uses the vocubulary well. The confidently judged "Interlude", a group of poems about Australia, shows that the poet does not require home soil or long-matured experience to write intelligently and plangently. Back in America, lines like these, about the eery shift of the physical senses after a power cut – "houses pinned // under their own dead weight" – are representative of a largely assured debut.

Nicholas Johnson's *Cleave* is a memorial to the recent devastating Foot and Mouth crisis and it makes transparent a number of patterns of work and life that had largely been concealed to urban folks like me: from the touchingly evoked (I almost said rendered) relationships between small-scale farmers and their livestock, to the angry revelation of the obvious contempt with which larger corporations view their animals. The occasional feyness in Johnson's poetry is plunged into body-shock, as lines like these show:

> I concentrate as blue lilies
> wrap around my throat and blend me in hives for
>   they are no longer
> lilies but cattle placenta

Johnson has a light touch. Within the broad heading of his remit (this book was a commission from South West Arts) Johnson incorporates a found poem written by his son undertaking a science experiment –

> I think sugar and salt dissolved because
> they were much smaller pieces so when
> they got wet they went soft and dissolved

– and tributes to Roy Fisher and David Gascoyne similarly find themselves in the countryside. None feels out of place, and, in the same way, Johnson's own autobiography is mingled with genuine polyphony, conveying the detailed human and animal complexity of the Foot and Mouth disaster.

It's interesting to see that Salt, with no public subsidy, has produced here three pleasurable and/or provocative reads, and that's less than a tenth of what Salt intends to produce each year on the same earn-your-keep/cross-fund basis. Johnson's Etruscan, with what seems to have been arms-length public funding, has produced a book of a similarly high standard in every way – all these books are printed and produced attractively, and I know each will reward re-reading. To be Bushesque, and risk trivialising the gruesome sights of *Cleave*: quite a few of these here new magic beans are worth the cow cost-analysis.

Hither and Thither, Wherever

MICHAEL CAINES

Bernard O'Donoghue, *Outliving*
Chatto & Windus, £8.99, ISBN 0701174811

LOVERS OF THE Big Poetry – of cosmic epics, scored with allusions to contemporary political strife and the difficult history of Mittel-Europa – perhaps regard a poet like Bernard O'Donoghue, with his eye for domestic details and a tendency to underplay his own importance, as a drip. Mythology and medieval literature come bedded down in his poems, as heroes ageing beneath their glorious summits or glanced at mid-adventure, or as castles retired out of modern history's reach. His verses, almost unstintingly described as lyrical, elegiac, humane and precise, are less concerned with the ocean than the drops that it unthinkingly engulfs. Reviewing *Here nor There* (1999) in the *TLS*, Michael O'Neill praised his knack for "eloquent dithering" with reference to the last line of "Westering Home": "Neither here nor there, and therefore home."

Outliving, O'Donoghue's fourth collection, begins and ends with a father's death, and the certainty of a new life – or at least the opportunity for rebirth. "The Day I Outlived My Father" plunges into being put out: "Yet no one sent me flowers, or even / asked me out for a drink." "So I am in new territory from here on", announces the second stanza, "must blaze my own trail . . .":

> at liberty at last like mad Arnaut
> to cultivate the wind, to hunt the bull
> on hare-back, to swim against the tide . . .

No confirmation follows, however, that any of this potential boldness is fulfilled, that the poet not only outlives his father but outdoes him. He is as hesitant as he was in the first stanza, "lacking maybe / the imagination to follow you / in investigating that other, older world". "The Mule Duignan", by contrast, is uncompromising about its rejection of a rural past:

> I hate that country:
> its poverties and embarrassments
> too humbling to retell. I'll never ever
> go back to offer it forgiveness.

This interrupts a childhood recollection of winter on the farm: "If the cow does die tonight, / we'll have to sell up and go." But the cow outlives expectation and "for the first and only time I saw / my parents embracing" – a reminder of one of O'Donoghue's best poems, "Ter Conatus", about a brother and sister living a humble farming life together for "nearly sixty years / . . . never touching once". One dies, and the other is left regretting that "He might have embraced her with a brother's arms" and never did. "The Mule Duignan", though, ends on a note of confident liberty: "[I] turned my back for ever on it all." ("As I hurried away, I took great care / not to turn back" he says elsewhere, half-ashamed to be too busy to explain something to a "man from Lauragh" who is "slow on the uptake".) Louis MacNeice's "Valediction" is a near notch away: "I cannot deny my past to which my self is wed, / The woven figure cannot undo its thread", but "I must go east and stay, not looking behind":

> I will acquire an attitude not yours
> And become one of your holiday visitors,
> And however often I may come
> Farewell, my country, and in perpetuum . . .

O'Donoghue returns MacNeice's sentiments without their hybrid pitch of Yeats and Auden, frequently casting himself as a "tourist in his own country", taking snapshots of the past and the idle present. He all but abolishes rhyme, perhaps unwilling to impede the line's unassertive, almost prosaic music, slipping occasionally into banality, but, on the whole, proving that big isn't necessarily clever. His book-ending and -starting poems lodge on the border between elegy for the dead and meditation for the living, also at home because neither here nor there.

Consistently and idiosyncratically, O'Donoghue the tourist-native takes tangential path from one thought to another with no guarantee that he will retrace his steps. "Trace

Elements" starts with "the outlaw Gisli" in need of a good disguise and ends with O'Donoghue's beard in the bin ("before it reminded somebody of something worse"). Several miniatures in *Outliving* riddle a pleasurable disquiet, and other brevities – such as "Artistic Block" and "Old Blue-Eyes" – show that the poet does not need to dig deep into his word-hoard to retrieve treasures. These are simple stories, exquisitely observed, "No more than that, yet everything / your eyes' attentiveness had reached out for".

They Might as well be English

JANE YEH

Richard Howard, *Trappings*
Arc, £7.95, ISBN 1900072343
J. D. McClatchy, *Division of Spoils*
Arc, £8.95, ISBN 1900072653
Dick Davis, *Belonging*
Banville, £7.95, ISBN 0856463485

INSTEAD OF OFFERING an insight into America's lively publishing scene, the latest entries in Arc's International Poets series (edited by John Kinsella) plough an all-too-familiar literary furrow. Writing within a tradition of lyric meditations and careful epiphanies, the poets in question – Richard Howard and J. D. McClatchy – might as well be English. While both teach at universities (Columbia and Yale, respectively), their affiliation with the academy shouldn't in itself label their work as staid or conventional. British suspicion of the "academic poetry" issuing from the States overlooks the fact that bards of wildly varying stripes hold university positions, from Leslie Scalapino and Ann Lauterbach to Charles Wright and Robert Hass. (Nor, as plenty of verse from the UK shows, do you have to be a professor to write dull poems.)

Originally published in America in 1999, Howard's eleventh collection, *Trappings*, showcases all the hallmarks of his style: the preoccupation with fine art ("Homage to Antonio Canaletto", "Eugène Delacroix: *Moorish Conversation*"), the wordplay and punning wit, the genteelly arch voice. Acclaimed for his translations of Baudelaire and Stendhal, in his own work Howard plays with issues of representation, what happens when the world is translated into art. The Delacroix poem shows the painter surreptitiously sketching a woman from afar: "He takes it all in as if / life were *the scene of the crime*". But his subject refuses to play dead – she sees him spying on her and watches him right back. Howard attempts to re-animate the sketch by inhabiting it from the sitter's perspective, a tactic repeated in further dramatic monologues about paintings. In "Family Values I-V", based on five different illustrations of Milton and his daughters, the girls tell a story of suffering and resentment not apparent from their portraits. Despite Howard's obvious enchantment with art, pictures, it seems, can record only outward appearances; it takes words – poetry – to capture reality.

An aesthete for whom literature and life are interchangeable, Howard declares, "Most of us ... / spoil our poems (our lives) because we have / ideas". Perhaps he should have heeded his own caveat a bit more. Though beguiling in conception, some of his pieces never reach beyond a kind of intellectual nattering, as if his imagination has been sandbagged by the weight of so much erudition. McClatchy's *Division of Spoils* looks similarly learned at first glance, with its borrowings from Proust, Shakespeare, and Horace, yet the pitch is more intimate, the approach plainly narrative. If Howard's mandarin style eventually disappoints because it lacks sufficient invention, McClatchy's straightforwardness masks defects of its own.

In selections from *The Rest of the Way* (1990) and *Ten Commandments* (1998), McClatchy ruminates tastefully on childhood memories, faltering relationships and his travels in the Middle East. Despite some unusual subject matter – the sonnet sequence "My Mammogram" finds the author having his distended breast scanned ("Fifty, male, already embarrassed") the strictly formal poems sound constrained, not complemented, by rhyme. An exception: the looser verse of "My Sideshow", in which McClatchy catalogues the circus freaks who fascinated him as a boy. Crucially arriving with the onset of puberty, the carnival comes to town one summer and lures him to its "World of Wonders":

> I kept staring at one jar. The thing inside seemed to float
> Up from a fishtail that was either leg or penis – or both.
> (I could hear my father now, outside the tent, calling me.)
>
> From its mouth, a pair of delicate legs emerged,
> As if it had swallowed a perfect twin. I gulped. Something
> Unspoken, then and since, rose like acid in my throat.

McClatchy might be better off leaving more things unspoken – his verbosity lends itself to easy conclusions, with any ambiguity muffled or tamed. His piece about a market stall in Jerusalem features morbidly accurate descriptions of goat heads (a meat prized by the poor) being cleaned for sale. Yet McClatchy can't resist adding that the heads "[b]ring to mind relief maps of the 'occupied / Territories'." (Thud.) He even spells out the Palestinian stallholder's plight: "Born on the wrong side / Of a new border, he's made / To carry his alien's ID". A professor with a deeper knowledge of the Middle East, the English-born Dick Davis spent several years in Iran and teaches at Ohio State University in America, where he translates Persian literature. His varied background, however, hardly informs the poems in *Belonging*, which strive to squeeze universal truths into simple quatrains and other rhymed forms. That there's a difference between clarity and banality seems to have escaped his notice, as the tidy little stanzas on "Growing Up", getting "Old" and having "Night Thoughts" attest. (The Larkinesque titles are deceptive; Davis's outlook is altogether cosier, his images substituting cliché for complexity.) Of old men – Davis is 58 – he opines, "What nags now at my mind / Is how they keep so kind, / Given the blows they bear, / And justified despair". The promisingly strange real-life tale of "Teresia Sherley", who left Persia in the seventeenth century to marry an English diplomat, inspires only generalisations about exile and displacement ("I'm neither here nor there"), in clunking tercets.

At least Davis treads more lightly in "West South West", a sonnet that hints at his intimations of mortality without shouting about them. Recalling how, as a child, he played at being Lord Nelson fighting the battle of Trafalgar, Davis subtly conveys his desire for "escape" (from school, from suburbia?). Decades later, he still hasn't got free: "I find I walk the shattered deck and wait / For when the marksmen see me, and take aim".

Bawheided, Badger-armed, Onward

ANDREW DUNCAN

Jeremy Hooker, *Adamah*
Enitharmon, £8.95, ISBN 1900564521
Robert Crawford, *The Tip of my Tongue*
Cape, £8.00, ISBN 0224069683

JEREMY HOOKER IS the author of two indispensable works on modern British poetry (*Poetry of Place* and *The Presence of the Past*) and holds a range of emotional attitudes – core Labour values, a wish for decentralisation of power from London, the importance of community, and of the transcendent and of vegetation cycles – which I would sign up to *in toto*. Is this why I find his poetry so banal?

> Norfolk in April drought:
>
> a cracked land.
>
> Where do we begin?
>
> Just here, say, at the point
> in the fields where you see
> the pinnacles of Salle church rise,
> and Cawston, the naked stub
> of the tower, and the roofs of Moor Farm.

Could it be worse? Isn't this the writer failing at his verbal task, cataloguing objects and relying on things which we find noble and tranquil in themselves? For large stretches of *Adamah*, Hooker is content to perceive what everyone perceives and say what everyone says. Is this left-wing authenticity?

His work on Richard Jefferies reminds us of his own poetry's tender evocation of rows of agricultural implements and of quiet rural places, and, indeed, reminds us that Georgian poetry was pretty much the translation of Jefferies' rural realism into short poems – giving rise to the cult of long country walks and of unemployed wood and brass impedimenta as pub decor. Like most conservatives, Hooker is converging from several points on one end: wherever he gets to is where we've already been.

Much of the book reaches for the mystic by deleting oppositions. (The result is similar to the work of the Georgian Andrew Young, an Anglican priest, in his long poem *Out of the World and Back*.) One such sequence, "Groundwork", was written as a collaboration with the sculptor Lee Grandjean, familiar perhaps as one of the "solutions" that Peter Fuller clutched at in his magnificent but unstable attempts to combine the boundless and sublime with revolutionary politics. When we read

> How many times
> the plough has gone through
> the soil

sped deep
in flinty loam

Christ alive
raised on
Adam's dust,
earth grassed
seeded
cropped

Word wrought in stone,
carved in wood

we can only sigh and ask what has gone wrong. Hooker seems to want the "deep past" and Norfolk churches, but no events or conflicts; it may be significant that when we are given isolated quotes from the exiled physicist David Bohm, we are not told that his position (which rejected quantum uncertainty and "idealism") was driven, quite essentially, by politics and the dialectic. Hooker offers us contentless beliefs. His eventless time aspires to mythical discourse, and he has written brilliantly on the mythical writers who, despite the theological problems, may be the most significant strand in the English literature of roughly 1930–60. Just as the mythographers owe more than can be told to the nineteenth-century Occult Revival, so also the best modern poetry is driven by Marxism, sexual awakening, and other radical toxins. What we find missing in Hooker is alienation. When you delete enough oppositions, everything becomes collective and interchangeable; and you have reached the banal again, by a roundabout path.

Robert Crawford has also written several books about the relationship between poets and place – the banal-transcendent; "place" may simply be a slow camera which denies short-term change and writes off human volition. My dream is to be given a wonderful Scottish book to review, so that I can say: get a load of this, sheepshanks! And here we are:

Red tiled roofs pave the village far below;

I clock the non-stop Colorado River,
Dandelion heads unblown in East Westphalia,

Bings, sunlit mesas of the Scottish Lowlands,
Stretching towards nettled woods whose watermills'

Dust harps, thick burr stones, and dark gavelocks
Promise half firlots or a grinding halt.

Crawford is not really fixed on place at all, but on flashing moments of alternative reality. (bing, spoil heap; gavelock, lever; firlot, a corn measure) He helped form, some twenty years ago, the Informationist group – although some say they really should have been named "morganatics" instead – and could be the Lloyd Cole of Scottish poetry – intellectual, enthusiastic, wonderfully suave. His equivalent of Lloyd's Country-and-Western roots could be the Christian message – this book starts with FIAT LUX and ends with "I am the

Light of the World". The preoccupation with information was really about the weakness of the ego when its barriers against an immersing, strange flood of perceptibles drop. The data light he bathes in is nothing less than the Word of God –and this verse is a starry-eyed praise song, like "if it should rain we'll let it!" He simply says yes to the world and its alternates. What is on "the tip of your tongue" is a neurological richness you can't quite grasp, where classification bursts and overflows, which is climactic and lingual – and is also the Ineffable, the majesty of God.

Crawford wants a soft map, where autonomous Scotland keeps heading North as England heads south. The dishonoured bond is twanged in the Gangs of New York-like "The Auld Enemy", where First Bawheid is probably "bollock-brain in chief", and the hostility of Scots to each other is contrasted with their sleek deference to Blair whenever it counts. Patriotism, generously, extends to an imaginary Scottish artist:

> Art-schooled at Wick Plein Air College,
> Our man chilled out with the Dunnet Head Group, then,
> Stateside, slaved as Jackson Pollock's cleaner.
> Slime obsessed him. Early works in salad cream and urine
>
> Date from this time, though his father ate most of them
> Immediately before his own death. Back home,
> Sketching at a Fife badger-baiting, the artist
> Lost his right arm, though he disliked the word "lost",
> Preferring to insist he knew exactly
> Where it had gone.

The Questionnaire

Poetry Review invited poets to reply to the question: "Which poet, or poets, have you been most surprised to enjoy?"

FRED D'AGUIAR

I should say of my chosen poet, Martin Carter of Guyana (1927-1997), that I have not been "surprised to enjoy" his work, but rather that his work continues to surprise me.

> is the university of hunger the wide waste.
> is the pilgrimage of man the long march.
> The print of hunger wanders in the land.
> The green tree bends above the long forgotten.
> ("University of Hunger", from *Poems of Resistance*, London 1954)

The intonation of the New Testament's Revelation; a rhetoric that is part-visionary, part-declamatory; a lower-case interrogative minus the expected question mark begging the questions of whose statement and in what English tongue; the elevated speech act on behalf of a hungry, homeless, forgotten underclass; all characterize this idea of deprivation as a politicising force. The result is poetry that is public and each poem declares an emergency.

These days it is hard to see writing as literally located on and in the margins far from the metropolitan centres. Most of the vocal and scribal subjects with vested interests in the margins, either through direct roots or political belief that is contra dominance by the centre, remain firmly ensconced in metropolises and thereby own lifelong subscriptions to globalisation. But for all of Martin Carter's writing life he lived and worked in the city of Georgetown. Guyana, a former British colony, won independence in 1966. Martin Carter made his name as a poet and public intellectual during the independence and nationalist movement of the 1950s. His poetry captured the tone of public concerns of the day. The British jailed him.

What were those concerns? Spurred by independence in India and then in Kenya, artists who were activists asked, "How can art best serve the nation-ideal?", conceived at the time as a distinct entity separate from Britishness. Nationalism is a crucible but a necessary one if a colony is to separate itself with even a modicum of success from the mother country. Martin Carter wrote his most famous poem, "University of Hunger" and several other great hits in ten published collections. He questioned the blind impetus towards the global and the cost to those located in the margins. Why isn't there a British edition of his poems?

Poet in the Gallery

MATTHEW WELTON

Formal Situations

Abstraction in Britain 1960–1970, Tate Liverpool.

WHILE IT MIGHT seem easy enough to accept the distinction usually made between representational and abstract art – that some paintings and sculptures are depictions of something outside of themselves and others are simply arrangements of colours and shapes – it is a distinction which relies on a couple of assumptions. The first has to do with the question of what it means for one thing to represent another; a question which implies the opposite question, of what it means for something not to represent anything else. The other assumption has to do with what "abstract" means. If something is described as abstract, then doesn't that suggest that there must be something else from which it is abstracted? Is it possible for something to be abstract in its own right?

The possibility of representation in art depends on, say, the image on the canvas being recognised as resembling something outside of itself, some person or thing that exists in the real world. This introduces the further possibility that the artist might see a likeness that the viewer doesn't get, or that the viewer might see things that the artist himself doesn't. It is easy to imagine either of these possibilities. And then there's the question of how far recognition depends on an individual's personal cultural experience. And then there's the question of whether ambiguity, after all, might in fact be a good thing in itself.

One difficulty with abstract art is that an image that doesn't look like something in the real world might still be a sort of representation – it is easy enough to imagine the splashy, dramatic work of the American Abstract Expressionists of the 1950s as representative of emotional or psychological states, for example – and this goes back to the problem of recognition. Another difficulty with describing a painting as "abstract" is that it implies that there is nothing really there.

The pamphlet produced by the Tate Liverpool to accompany this exhibition talks about the preoccupation twentieth-century artists had with purifying art – about "the desire to [...] eliminate representation and instead to address those characteristics which define the work of art as a thing *in itself*". This suggests that it is possible for a completed work of art to be neither a function of how the artist or the viewer sees it but to be simply the thing that it is.

Taking this approach removes the need to see art as either representational or abstract. Instead, when viewed as a thing in itself, it makes more sense to describe art as *literal*, or *actual*; not representational but *presentational*. At which point it is necessary to move the focus from what art might refer to, to what art is composed of. This most obviously suggests the materials used, but – since considerations like colour, composition, line and proportion are not a matter of recognition – it can be interpreted to include the way in which those materials are arranged. And here the artist becomes confronted with the liberty and responsibility of coming up with something which in itself is art.

The works in this show which seem to bear this responsibility most rigorously and most comfortably are the half-dozen pieces by Michael Kidner. Made of gouache or crayon and pencil on paper, these compositions are simply areas of colour, arranged in blocks and separated by gentle, squiggly lines. None of them is much more than half a metre in height. Their titles – "Red and Olive Wave" or "Wavy Stripe: Green, Blue, Orange, Red", for example – are the simplest descriptions of what the images are and, as such, don't seem to have any idea of any significance beyond themselves. In fact, there is a kind of humility in the way the pencil lines are left visible – maybe like in a mathematical equation where the workings are not rubbed out? – so that in their slight untidiness the pictures become even simpler. Similarly, the crayon does look like crayon, making the surfaces sort of blotchy and uneven. The heavy-looking, yellowing paper emphasises that these images are just things that were made, and that it is the way that they are made that makes them art. Part of the achievement is in the colours that are used, and in the relation between these colours; and there's also something in the unfussy geometric arrangements, and how they make use of proportion and shape.

There are similar things going on in the wall of screenprints by John Hoyland. Using simple contrasts of blues and reds or blues and greens, these pieces also present the viewer with generally simplistic formal structures, though they are perhaps less geometrically precise. The compositions are like investigations into colour and line, section and proportion, with the black colours at the edges reacting with the larger blocks of colour in the centre. In being made with paper and being no more than poster-size, there is something unostentatious in Hoyland's work that seems to make it more real. That these are screenprints adds to this effect – while what is on display might be the more successful of a series of experiments, there is still the possibility that there will be others that aren't shown.

Perhaps there is something in the fact that these two groups of work are presented as series that makes them feel more realised than much of the work on display here. In showing each piece alongside a small number of others similar to it, the work seems more relaxed about occupying the space it is given. Another effect of this is that the work feels like a part of something greater. Which might simply be the process by which each series was created, or which might be the larger context – the *world?* the *art world?* – in which any work will have to find its place.

The other striking work here is Bridget Riley's "Nineteen Greys". This piece is itself made up of four pieces – large, almost glossy squares covered with small, off-circular shapes. As the title suggests, only grey is used, though the shades of it vary from something cloud-coloured to something bluish. Geometry again is an obvious consideration, though the effect here is more subtle and more clever. By a restrained playfulness this piece achieves a kind of optical trick that gives the image a deceptive sense of texture.

One significant difference between the Riley piece and the Kidners and the Hoylands is that "Nineteen Greys" feels a little slicker and, in a way, more conventionally complete. This might have to do with the fact that there are no remaining pencil-marks; or maybe there is more to it than that. To bring about the optical effect, which is achieved with colour and shape here, requires some amount of working-out before the actual painting is made. For sure, it is not unusual for an artist to make preparatory sketches, and, in a painting like this, that preparation still feels present. But this relationship between a work of art and the way that it is made has some tricky implications for a lot of the other exhibits.

The pieces so far mentioned are the exceptions in a show where the canvases are generally huge. And often the most affecting thing about these two- and three-metre paintings is simply their size, the area of canvas covered in paint. To accept the idea that a painting is a thing in itself, is to accept the use of scale as a legitimate technique. So perhaps it isn't just size that causes the problem here. What is most unconvincing about much of this work is that it feels like it got to what it is by way of a short-cut, that it arrived on the canvas without having travelled to get there. There is the sense that too often the artists took account of what a finished abstract painting looks like – huge, slabby colour-blocks on huge, slabby canvases – and just went ahead and made them, and that was that. Any sense that a painting is the history of its own making – the way in which art is the working-out of itself – feels like it was ignored in the hurry to get the work made. So there is a way in which this kind of work really is abstract: that it is abstracted from the impulse with which its making began.

But if the work in this show is put into context, then the inclusion of some of the less convincing pieces becomes more understandable. That this exhibition features British work from the 1960s means that these artists were working at a time of significant cultural shifts. Most pertinently, as the pamphlet mentions, the 1959 Tate exhibition of Abstract Expressionist work, *The New American Painting*, had suddenly presented British artists with a new understanding of the non-representational potential of art. But simply producing work that resembles that of Rothko or Pollock is like borrowing a blueprint but not bothering with the prototype. It can mean forgoing the essential processes through which those more radical artists worked. And if art is to be taken as something actual and non-representational then, whichever materials are used, it is the method by which it is made that has to be got exactly right.

Artists' Notes

Billy Childish is a cult figure in America, Europe, and Japan. In a twenty year period he has published 30 collections of his poetry, recorded over 90 full-length, independent LPs, and produced over 2000 paintings. Born in 1959 in Chatham, Kent, Childish left Secondary education at 16 an undiagnosed dyslexic. Refused an interview at the local art school, he entered the Naval Dockyard at Chatham as an apprentice stonemason. During the following six months (the artist's only prolonged period of employment), he produced some six hundred drawings in "the tea huts of hell". On the basis of this work he was accepted into St Martin's School of Art to study painting. He was expelled before completing the course. He has since spent some 12 years "painting on the dole", developing his own highly personal writing style, and producing his art independently. For more information please contact **www.billychildish.com** or **www.hangmanbooks.com**

David Godbold was a "Rome Scholar" in residence at the British School at Rome from July to September 2002. The drawings reproduced here are from a series of 44 small works made during that period. Godbold makes drawings via a complex process of quotation, and the "Rome Drawings" function on three levels. First, the background of the drawings are found papers, discarded in the Rome area. Second, the images placed on top are responses to life's immediate and everyday occurrences.The "Rome Drawings" consciously employ imagery influenced by Renaissance master drawings. Third, the artist habitually uses text, the texts making reference to various kinds of cultural activity from philosophy to Reality TV. Godbold's work is extensively collected, and is reproduced here courtesy of Rhodes + Mann, London. For more information visit **www.rhodesmann.com**

Letters to the Editors

AM I ALONE in detecting a recent spate of high-profile rumblings, all bemoaning the superabundance of writers over readers (eg *Acumen* 46, editorial)? Such "news" has limited bombshell value for poets who, in witnessing the collapse of Oxford Poets and successive waves of purdah concerning grassroots poetry distribution in bookshops, have demonstrated a mastery of Zen of truly cosmic proportions. Indeed, wherever free wine is to be had, poets can be found chuckling in a decidedly free-spirited manner over a long-standing rumour that at least eighty per cent of all poetry sales can be traced to a solitary octogenarian in Bradford. And he buys mostly Heaney. Never mind. Think of all the compensations. Patricia Oxley's tongue-in-cheek comment "Shut down the creative writing classes, open the creative reading sessions" isn't as ironic – or as undesirable – as it might first seem. How richly unco it would be to find yourself, in a few years' time, applying for an Arts Council New Readers' Award. Hard cash (tax-free) for those who have read one book, but need support in order to make their way through the next. Just imagine the shelves of the newly refurbished Poetry Library crammed with titles like *Readers' News* and *The Readers' and Artists' Yearbook*. And all those cheap little box-adverts popping up everywhere urging you to consider the simple-enough question: "Why Not be a Reader? (and your money back if you don't actually read something in public by the end of the courses)". Of course, there's a serious issue at the back of all of this; but I suspect it has far less to do with numbers of writers as with the current concerns of our culture and of its poets. A contributing factor here is a "faux esoterism" in much recent poetry. As Adrian Mitchell puts it: "Most people ignore most poetry because most poetry ignores most people". Not that I'm for accessibility at all costs; I genuinely celebrate our "difficult" poets. But I also celebrate the likes of Billy Collins, Jackie Kay and Henry Shukman, because without being simplistic or fake they write books you can give to just about anyone. They'll probably get read all the way through. And – yes – they might even inspire someone to write something themselves? Yuk! Phwar! God forbid.

Mario Petrucci
Royal Literary Fund Fellow
Oxford Brookes University

HAVING JUST FINISHED reading the Spring issue of *PR* I note your exhortation that you would like to receive letters intended for publication.

The new *Poetry Review* is really different in kind from its predecessor. A brief list of these differences, as I see them, is as follows:

Layout and presentation. It's now simple and uncomplicated – poems, essays, reviews, art. The readability of the journal is thus improved at a stroke. The previous format (or lack of) was simply a mishmash.

The new *PR* is intelligent, and respects the intelligence of its readers. It is well informed but no longer plays for safety. We now hear news of J. H. Prynne and Keston Sutherland; the extraordinary Kelvin Corcoran gets a mention in an article alongside Denise Riley. This indicates a decisive shift, an acknowledgement that poetry involves risk.

And are we hearing less of Poets in Residence at the new Wembley Stadium with ra-ra cheerleaders already climbing into their glitzy raffia skirts in anticipation? Is it that the editors on the new *PR* expect its readers to be grown up?

Finally – and I'm not sure what the ingredients are here – the journal is exciting. Names that are quite new to me – Robert Stein, for example – are clearly producing work of considerable power. Whatever the pungent ingredients, the outcome is the result of editorial care.

This is not to knock the work of Peter Forbes. His services to poetry and the contribution made by *Poetry Review* to English letters hardly need commendation from the likes of me. But the old *Poetry Review* had grown tired, tired and safe.

Yours sincerely,

Alex Smith

In the year ending April 2003, subscriptions to *Poetry Review* increased by over 20% on the previous year. A big thank you to all our new readers, and to those subscribers who continue to enjoy the magazine.